Webcam

Webcam

Daniel Miller and
Jolynna Sinanan

polity

First published in 2014 by Polity Press

Polity Press
65 Bridge Street
Cambridge CB2 1UR, UK

Polity Press
350 Main Street
Malden, MA 02148, USA

ISBN-13: 978-0-7456-7146-8
ISBN-13: 978-0-7456-7147-5 (pb)

A catalogue record for this book is available from the British Library.

Typeset in 11 on 13 pt Sabon
by Toppan Best-set Premedia Limited
Printed and bound in Great Britain by Clays Ltd, St Ives PLC

For further information on Polity, visit our website: www.politybooks.com

Contents

Acknowledgements

Daniel Miller would like to thank Stefana Broadbent, who first suggested this topic, Natalie Wright, who worked as an intern for him on this project, and the various students and friends who provided him with pilot interviews. Support at the Department of Anthropology UCL, especially from Susanne Küchler, the Head of Department, is gratefully acknowledged. Thanks also for support from the Royal Melbourne Institute of Technology (RMIT), where he has been appointed Adjunct Professor, School of Media and Communication.

Jolynna Sinanan would like to thank Tania Lewis and the School of Media and Communication at RMIT and UCL for funding her fieldwork in Trinidad. Thank you also to Heather Horst, and to Miley and Toffee, Zaid, Guruh and Tamara for their boundless generosity and hospitality.

We are both immensely grateful to the people of El Mirador who gave so much thought and time to assist us in our work. We apologize for the fact that, given our promise of anonymity, we cannot thank them individually. We would also like to thank those who made comments on the manuscript, Sheba Mohammid, Razvan Nicolescu, Anna Pertierra, Marisa Wilson, assistance from Mary Gray and the two anonymous reviewers for Polity.

1

Conclusion: A Theory of Attainment

Skype and webcam

The grounds for choosing the topic of webcam in personal communications were really quite simple. It was evident from research on other new communication technologies that webcam was coming to play a significant role. Yet, we knew of no anthropological studies dedicated to ascertaining its consequences. By 2011, Skype was reaching a critical point. Not ubiquitous, at least compared to mobile phones, but because of large-scale initiatives such as 'One laptop per child' with their integrated webcams, access was spreading to include lower income populations (Rosenberg, 2012). In Trinidad today, most people have transnational friends or family, which seemed to be the most common initial incentive for using Skype. Our research suggested that for some relationships, webcam had become a critical intervention. We also felt confident that webcam was now sufficiently embedded as an accepted part of people's everyday lives here to become the subject of ethnography as a study of the mundane.

Although we undertook the study from a hunch that the impact of webcam might now be profound, we didn't start with any particular ideas or hypotheses. We are not that kind of natural scientist. We began, instead, from what we hope is the modesty of anthropology that says the expertise lies not with the academic, but with the peoples they study. It is their creativity and inventiveness, their interpretations and accommodations, their insights and frustrations that we must share; and from them build a picture, a generalized image of what seems to be happening in their world. Only then do we ask why this matters for anthropologists and indeed for everyone.

The title of this book, *Webcam*, is problematic for various reasons, but we would argue it is simply better than the alternatives. Many of our informants, especially in the UK, avoid the term altogether, because a critical moment in the spread of webcam came with its usage for pornography as by 'camgirls' (Senft, 2008). Another influential initial usage was setting up a webcam to observe a site such as a street or events such as a rare bird nesting. Apart from within the last chapter, we do not cover such uses of webcam. You should assume a silent sub-title Webcam – but in most chapters only as used within personal communications. These communications may be dyadic or between groups as, for example, when two families greet each other at Christmas. So our interest is closer to that of Baym (2010) and Broadbent (2012) but very different from Senft (2008). To avoid these earlier connotations of the term, many people prefer to refer instead to proprietary platforms such as Skype and FaceTime, and terms such as Skyping or 'do you want to Skype?' are universally used and recognized. But there are various such platforms, so that we could not use any one of these for our title. By now, many other informants are comfortable with the term webcam and will themselves extend this to create the verbs 'webcamming' or 'to webcam', for example, often interchangeably with Skyping (which is in any case confusing since half of Skype calls are made without webcam). Given the rise of FaceTime and webcam within smartphones, the term webcam may grow at the expense of Skype. So we concluded that *Webcam* was the imperfect, but best available title for this volume. In the final chapter, we will move beyond personal communication to issues of surveillance and the use of webcams in commerce more generally.

Whatever our title, we still need to acknowledge the sheer dominance of Skype in the use of webcam for personal communication up till now. Skype, the product of two Estonian developers, was released in 2003. Incredibly, by 2005, it was bought by eBay for US$2.6 billion and subsequently by Microsoft in 2011 for US$8.5 billion. Still more than a third of its development team are based in Estonia. Currently, it is being incorporated into Microsoft with the migration of Windows Messenger into Skype. According to Skype's Chief Technology Strategist, by the end of 2012 Skype accounted for around 25 per cent of all international calls of any kind (Rosenberg, 2012). Around half of these Skype calls employed video. The average call was around half an hour and there are around 40 million users online at peak times. Skype has been downloaded approximately 200 million times on iPhone and Android phones. According to *Skype Numerology* (Mercier, 2012), the number of monthly paying Skype users is a mere 8.1 million, leaving revenues remaining sparse at an estimated US$400 million per annum. Skype is, however, likely to enhance future products and add to the Microsoft range in various ways.

This is not, however, a study of either Skype or webcam merely as a technology or commercial product. It is an anthropological study of its role in relationships. Consider the following quotation from our pilot study: 'You know what men are like, they are so impatient with technology. They get so easily frustrated and angry. And to be honest, webcam in those days was pretty crap, kept cutting off, out of focus, just starting a conversation and it goes wrong.' This is hardly a unique complaint; in many of our conversations, we included some discussion about people's first experiences with webcam and these were fairly mixed. On reflection, we are rather glad that we waited until 2011 in order to carry out our research. We have the feeling that the whole thing is a rather more pleasant engagement by now. So why start with this vignette? It makes the point that people have relationships with people and they have relationships with technology, and, mostly, we can't really disentangle the two. This affair ended soon after. Did their frustration with the technology cause, add merely a soupçon, or was it irrelevant to that break up? In thereby conforming to her general stereotypes of what men are like, did this experience increase his masculine attraction as a proper man, or demonstrate that he was exactly the kind of man who was really not for her? Are such stereotypes best regarded as general, regional or individual?

If there is a dominant topic within anthropology it is, and probably should be, the study of relationships. Anthropologists recognize that there are no unmediated, pure relationships. All the ways in which relationships exist, including communication, are cultural activities. The peoples whom anthropologists encounter in Melanesia or Amazonia prove just as fraught as the anthropologists themselves with anxiety and regrets about what they have just said, which for them might include its conformity with religious scruples, politeness with respect to that particular relationship and all those myriad filters that make certain that so much must remain unsaid and that communication is replete with constraint and misunderstanding. Even in our digitally founded world, the technological can often be the least significant aspect of mediation. So before we can approach our topic of webcam, we need to establish how we understand this concatenation of the human, culture and technology.

This is one of the reasons why this book has a slightly unusual structure. We will start with our conclusions. The next section is called 'A Theory of Attainment'. The intention is firstly to take responsibility for these issues regarding how we contend with this inevitable mix of technical and cultural properties. The remaining chapters consist largely of reportage from interviews and ethnography, followed by analysis, leading to these conclusions. But we felt it was important to be able to judge those conclusions against these more substantive materials, which means being clear as to the claims we intend to make. Finally, we wanted to establish the academic grounds for asking readers to then submit themselves to so much detailed discussion of material mostly derived from a small town in Trinidad, which otherwise is unlikely to be of much concern. For all these reasons, this chapter starts with our conclusions.

A theory of attainment

> Most persons are surprised, and many distressed, to learn that essentially the same objections commonly urged today against computers were urged by Plato in the *Phaedrus* (274–7) and in the *Seventh Letter* against writing. Writing, Plato has Socrates say in the *Phaedrus*, is inhuman, pretending to establish outside the mind what in reality can be only in the mind. It is a thing, a manufactured product. The same of course is said of computers. Secondly, Plato's Socrates urges, writing destroys memory. Those who use writing will become forgetful, relying on an external resource for what they lack in internal resources. Writing weakens the mind. (Ong 1982: 78)

The conclusions of this book are in several respects the exact opposite of what may be found in most popular writing regarding the impact and consequences of new communication media. The problem is that there is a natural tendency to take the world we live in at any particular moment as the bedrock of our authenticity, a world that has come to appear natural, or at least natural in comparison to the changes that are about to occur to us. The quotation from Ong reveals that for Plato's Socrates, the invention of writing meant that we could no longer be fully human; the essential qualities of our mind, our creativity, our memory and, above all, our authenticity were forever lost. Ong notes that in the fifteenth century, very similar arguments were made about the invention of printing, which would downgrade the wisdom of persons in favour of the products of the machine. Today, the ability to write has become so ubiquitous that we have almost forgotten that it is a technology and when anthropologists tell us about societies without writing, we are more tempted to consider that it is they, rather than us, who lack an essential quality of being fully human. To be illiterate is now regarded as pitiful, rather than the superior version of humanity presumed by Plato.

Any new media is first experienced as an additional and problematic *mediation* to our lives. We can't help but contrast it with some imagined conversation between two people standing in a field as representing the original, unmediated and natural form of communication. A technology, by contrast, is always regarded as something artificial that imposes itself between the conversationalists and *mediates* that conversation. An example of this kind of discourse is the recent book by Turkle, *Alone Together* (2011). The book is, in essence, a lament for a passing world of *real* relationships based on true social life that are most fully established by face-to-face communication – a world that is lost by the more superficial and mediated world of digital communication. Her inclusion of advances in robotics reinforces the idea that recent technological advances are leading to a loss of something essential about humanity. The problem we have with such books lies in thinking that a relationship to a robot represents a downgrading of our humanity because it substitutes for a *real* relationship. Amongst the many things this ignores is history. Not many Christians would have a problem seeing Jesus as a friend, nor would they regard a nun who takes vows of separation as a pathology. English people sometimes seem to prefer the friendship of pets to people. Material culture is an anthropological study of relationships to material things, such as our house, that may be amongst our key relationships. There has never been a time when people reduced their relationships merely to other people. While in some ways unprecedented, in other respects, digital technologies still have a very long way to go before they reach the degree of *extraordinary* found in the relationships presumed by religious cosmologies, created (or recognized as utterly real, depending upon one's personal religiosity) by humanity.

It is not easy to refute writings such as Turkle, which tend to be hugely popular, because they resonate with a lament for past authenticity, which is a leitmotif of the modern world, as it was often in ancient worlds (consider the Roman satirist Juvenal). Perhaps the worst terms found in the discussion of new digital technologies are words such as 'real' and 'true' when used to describe the prior status quo. These resonate with popular assumptions which are almost universally held, and constantly reinforced in journalism. New technologies are making humanity itself more artificial and thereby less intrinsically human. The discourses that prevail, both popular and academic, are essentially conservative discourses.

In stark contrast to such arguments is the reiteration of a tenet of anthropological theory that is found in the recent introduction to the book *Digital Anthropology*, written by Miller and Horst (2012: 12). With respect to these arguments, they suggest that

> This is entirely antithetical to what anthropological theory actually stands for. In the discipline of anthropology all people are equally cultural, that is the products of objectification. Australian indigenous tribes may not have much material culture, but instead they use their own landscape to create extraordinary and complex cosmologies that then become the order of society and the structures guiding social engagement (e.g., Munn, 1973; Myers, 1986). In anthropology, there is no such thing as pure human immediacy; interacting face-to-face is just as culturally inflected as digitally mediated communication but, as Goffman (1959, 1975) pointed out again and again, we fail to see the framed nature of face-to-face interaction because these frames work so effectively.

The discussion concludes with a principle. 'Digital anthropology will be insightful to the degree it reveals the mediated and framed nature of the nondigital world. Digital anthropology fails to the degree it makes the nondigital world appear in retrospect as unmediated and unframed. We are not more mediated simply because we are not more cultural than we were before' (Miller and Horst, 2012: 13).

In other words, anthropology as a discipline rejects the idea that two people standing in a field, or two Australian indigenous individuals conversing in the desert, are in any way closer to some natural foundation for conversation than two people discussing their relationship through Facebook. Even in the desert, these indigenous individuals converse in a world highly structured by the appropriate and customary forms of address for the kinship categories they occupy. They spoke as a mother's brother should to a sister's son, and may well have assumed that their conversations were being influenced by spirits and ancestors. We do not see their ancestors, just as we don't see the infrastructure behind Facebook, but the possibility that the unseen may determine what we can and should say are equally strong.

Goffman (1959) did more than anyone to refute the illusion of communication as natural and unmediated. He revealed the myriad ways in which our everyday appearance and everyday encounters are the products of artifice. We literally compose ourselves before entering the door. This 'we' was not people within digital worlds but the folk in rural areas such as the Shetland Islands. The very people we laud as models of authenticity, artisanal craftspeople in weaving wool, were actually found to be crafting themselves more or less continuously. Self-presentation was discovered to be the art of everyday life.

But the very fact that Goffman's work came across as a revelation is testimony to the degree to which we do not easily view either our own or others' worlds in this manner. Goffman does not often impute intentionality to this activity; we can't help but act in this way. Indeed, it is this lack of consciousness that has allowed us to conceive of personal communication as natural and unmediated. Goffman also showed how frames that cue us into what kind of behaviour is expected of that particular context help us remain unselfconscious about the way we behave differently in these different contexts. We naturally (that is highly artificially) act differentially when we are within a theatre or while on holiday (Goffman, 1975). Much of Miller's previous work on material culture (2009a, 2009b), reinforced by the huge contribution of the anthropologist Bourdieu (1984), has been an examination of how objects such as clothing or housing act as frames in Goffman's sense, telling us how to behave without us realizing that this is the effect they are having upon us. One of the arguments of the next chapter is that the experience of having a webcam is analogous to the experience of having to read the work of Goffman. Both lead to an increasing consciousness and self-consciousness about the frames of human interaction. We are not more or less framed, but when we are looking at a rectangular computer screen right in front of us, we may certainly be more aware of the degree to which personal communication works within frames.

Both digital technologies and academic work such as *Digital Anthropology* help give us an appreciation of Goffman's insight that communication always was framed. An example of this could be van Dijck's (2007) book *Mediated Memories in the Digital Age*. This examines the impact of a whole slew of new media on memory. Certainly, there are marked changes. Photography seems to be turning into a more transient phenomenon for immediate circulation on social networking sites. These and blogs help to synchronize experience amongst a social group. Music may change in its relationship to nostalgia. Far from acting largely as an instrument of dematerialization, digital forms add considerably to this external capacity to store memory outside of the self in multimodal, more collective forms. Memory has become even more about looking things up on search engines, rather than some pure act of introspection. Indeed, when considering the totality of new digital forms, this feeds a kind of collective fantasy of the digital memory machine that one day will be able to encapsulate the entirety of our externalized memory genres.

Certainly, there is a clear development in the facilitation of memory as lodged in forms outside of the mind – we all have a bigger external hard drive – the process that was lamented by Plato, though without that particular analogy. But the key point made by this book is that all these developments are actually useful in helping to confirm that memory was never the highly individualized cognitive function that existed primarily within an individual's brain. Following Bergson (2007 [1912]), Halbwachs (1992) and others, van Dijck (2007) argues that memory is far more collective and normative than we have acknowledged. It is socially incumbent upon us to video our babies' first attempts to walk. The way Facebook and other media then create a more collective sense of memory is in some measure returning us to this more socialized and less individualized memory of most of human history. Once again, the digital isn't taking memory into post-human realms, but is helping refine our comprehension of the prior mediations within human memory. Goody's (1987) research on the invention of both literacy and writing leads to similar observations about the way these impacted upon our capacity for recall, the recapitulation of stories and the nature of our sociality. But as an anthropologist, Goody also stressed the importance of understanding these changes at the level of cultural norms rather than the psychology of individual competence. Goody's writing is particularly pertinent because a problem with this refutation of conservatism is that it could be read as an opposition to the very concept of change itself. If we cannot become more mediated, then does that mean the impact of these new technologies is inevitably insignificant? Goody (1977, 1987) is quite forthright in acknowledging that the changes brought about by technologies such as writing and printing are fundamental, indeed, foundational to the emerging domination of various forms of reason. Ong (1982: 81) agrees: 'Like other artificial creations and indeed more than any other, it is utterly invaluable and indeed essential for the realization of fuller, interior, human potentials. Technologies are not mere exterior aids but also interior transformations of consciousness.' As Goody (1977) suggests, it would be absurd to dismiss the rise of science, for example, as other than fundamental in terms of human capacity and this is clearly a cultural and indeed global phenomenon, not reducible to the comparison of one individual's mind to another, which is why psychology is likely to be of little help here. Anthropology can retain cultural sensitivity while still appreciating that we simply must contend with long-term change. We have developed our theory of attainment precisely in order to deal with this quandary. How can we both acknowledge that technological developments may fundamentally change humanity while at the same time reject the idea that they are making us more or less human?

It is vital to the future of the discipline of anthropology, then, that we find a language that casts the savage mind as neither more primitive nor more authentic than the literate or, what Goody (1977) calls, the domesticated mind. Because, at the other end of the spectrum are those who would argue that it is only through digital technologies that we have finally become properly human. These arguments tend to start from a more psychological or philosophical liberalism, where humanity is the individual person who has now been extended into something else thanks to new technology. The highly influential media theorist Marshall McLuhan called one of his books *Understanding Media: The Extensions of Man* (1964). One of his arguments was: 'Rapidly we approach the final phase of the extension of man – the technological simulation of consciousness, when the creative process of knowing will be collectively and corporately extended to the whole of human society, much as we have already extended our senses and our nerves by the various media' (pp. 3–4). The idea of the individual as now technologically extended, or even upgraded through the development of new digital media, gains new traction in various notions of the cyborg, the trans- and the post-human (e.g., Whitehead and Wesch, 2012).

Just as Turkle's conservatism is echoed in much of the population, so is this enticement of the new. Such ideas are popular amongst many of our young informants, because it is these digital natives (Palfrey and Glasser, 2008) who are likely to already see it as a matter of 'nature' that texting on a smartphone, for example, is obviously more sensible and authentic than its precedents, with more chance to consider and reply at convenience. For them, the previous technology, for example, the landline phone call, is positively barbaric, being clunky, intrusive and constraining. They regard the prior period of technology as not closer to nature, but further from nature, a series of awkward and deficient technologies that they are only too glad to get away from. Parents are awkward attempts at humanity, a state which is only properly realized in their children's facility with the new digital world and the full realization of human potentiality. The geeky youths living their lives primarily online would be just as dismissive of Turkle, as a poor apology for a proper human being, as she might be of them.

Miller and Horst (2012) insist that we are not more mediated, but that the nature of mediation is certainly subject to change. It follows that we need to find a means of understanding the impact of new technologies that allows us to consider these as radical changes in consciousness and other basic modes of life, but without this being seen as either an increase or decrease in our essential humanity. We want to retain an anthropological sensibility of diversity and change in humanity as something comparative but not better or worse, more or less. It is because these issues are so fundamental, and it is so easy to slip into these languages of conservatism or futurism, that we propose to give our perspective the otherwise pretentious title of a 'theory', though it clearly does not fulfil the technical requirements of the term. So *theory* as in our colloquial use of that word. We call this 'A Theory of Attainment'. The principle that mediation is an intrinsic condition of being human provides one leg for our theory to stand upon.

The other leg is derived from an earlier book Miller wrote with Slater in 2000, called *The Internet: An Ethnographic Approach*. That book, like the present one, was concerned to theorize a new media – the internet – and to consider the nature of change that resulted from its adoption, using the island of Trinidad for its case study. It argued for a four-phase approach to the study of new media. Unfortunately, it also developed four rather cumbersome labels for these phases, which Miller now rather regrets. The first was called the *expansive realization*. This label was used to argue that people who have access to a new media are at first usually concerned to use this technology to facilitate things they already had been trying to do, but had up to then been thwarted by the lack of means. Only once these are accomplished do they tend to address more unprecedented uses. People already had the ambition to search information more easily, and the internet provides the means. The emphasis here is on a human condition, which is in some ways always in a situation of incompleteness with respect to what we want to be or do. The world is always, amongst other things, frustrating. This suggests that humanity includes a latency that may be realized thanks to technological facilitation. We wonder what it would be like to visit and see the planet Saturn but we can't, as yet. We would like to see family members who are now living on the other side of our own planet, and thanks to webcam we can.

While it is likely that a new technology will be used to facilitate something people already knew they wanted, this is not what makes the result attainment, for the purposes of our theory. Attainment is not intended to be considered as achievement. It is the next phase, when this facility becomes the merely taken-for-granted condition of what people simply presume as an integral aspect of who they are, which is the realization of what we are calling attainment. The ability to write is a mark of attainment because we now tend to view those without that ability as though they lacked some fundamental property of being ordinarily human. Originally writing was an achievement, but by now it is considered a necessary condition. For many people, being able to type on a computer, or to drive a car, or speak on a telephone has become a similar mark of attainment. Webcam will serve as an exemplification of this process because of the sheer speed with which it passes from an ideal we had aspired to, to a mundane technology that we take for granted.

If we combine these two perspectives, we can see how they point away from humanity as a position of prior authenticity, or a given condition, by focusing instead on humanity as a project that is never complete, but always in various ways frustrated by lack of means, or exhibiting the hubris of complaisant acceptance of the munificence of science. A Theory of Attainment is one in which we refuse to view a new technology as disrupting some prior holistic or ideal state. The word 'attain' implies that, although it was not previously achievable, it was already latent in the condition of being human. The cultural use of the technology derives in large measure from the desires of populations and is not simply a necessary consequence of the invention of that particular device. After a while, the same technology is likely to stimulate new aspirations which will be as yet unattained. The concept of attainment therefore provides us with a humanity that is neither intrinsically conservative, nor fully realized in some utopian future. It is, rather, a humanity that incorporates its own potential for change and highlights our capacity for those changes to become merely normative with quite extraordinary speed.

Some caveats are in order here. Just because we aspire to something doesn't mean it is axiomatically good that some new technology has allowed us to fulfil that desire. Guns, and indeed all weapons, are clearly forms of attainment that realize a human capacity for violence and murder, and allow this to attain possibilities of mass destruction that would not otherwise have been possible. They are attainments because, as anyone reading the Bible would have to acknowledge, humanity has always been able to envisage the mass destruction of whole populations. It was just rather harder to slaughter them one by one than to drop an atomic weapon on them. Similarly, Schüll's (2012) recent study of machine gambling in Las Vegas is chilling in its portrayal of what we can use machines to reduce people into being, but again slavery, whether to machines or to other people, is clearly an entirely human capacity that was commonly practised in the past with limited technical resources. So the theory of attainment should not be judgemental.

This clearly gives us a problem with regard to the word 'attain' which does tend to connote positive accomplishment. We would have preferred a word that connotes the ability of technology to quickly become something taken for granted as a human capacity but without seeing this as necessarily positive. As with the case of choosing *Webcam* for the title of our book, *attainment* is imperfect but simply the best word we could find. Our informants are full of value judgements about what they regard as positive and negative about webcam. We report and discuss their judgements. By contrast, we are trying to steer our course between the Scylla of conservatism and the Charybdis of techno-liberation, and have no desire to founder on either side. For this reason, we would ask you to hold judgement on our theory of attainment. It is really only at the end of this book, when we return it to its proper place as the conclusion of our ethnographic investigation, that we will achieve our aim of seeing attainment neither as positive nor negative but merely a theory of how technology becomes an ordinary aspect of being routinely human.

The other caveat is brought out best in Fukuyama's (2003) book about the post-human. We may want to reject the language of the post-human with respect to these new digital media, but that can only work if we simultaneously acknowledge at least the theoretical possibility that a line can be breached which challenges our concept of the human. Fukuyama argues as follows: if we see Prozac as similar to the drug *soma* imagined in Huxley's *Brave New World* (2005), then have we reached a condition that is similar enough to Huxley's dystopian vision that a term such as post-human is warranted. Our own view, in opposition to Fukuyama, is that the term post-human is not helpful. The issues are simply clearer if we try instead to retain a boundary which states either someone is human or is not human. It is clear that some of the bodily and mental transformations discussed by Fukuyama could lead to such a massive alteration of our condition that we should not regard the result as human at all.

Indeed, his discussions around the definition of being human in relation to human rights suggest that these are quite similar to current arguments about abortion. At what point should a foetus be described legally and morally as human as against non-human (Oaks, 1994; Gammeltoft, 2003)? Should an animal be accorded rights and how do these compare with those we regard as appropriate to a human being? We briefly note this point, which lies outside the scope of this enquiry, in order to acknowledge that a rounded theory of attainment would also include discussion of the point at which we would no longer be talking about a theory of attainment because the result is not human, but perhaps a robot, for example. Theoretically, Turkle could be right in suggesting a new technology takes us beyond a state we could regard as properly human. We don't want to use our theory of attainment to reject this as a theoretical possibility; we simply want to attest that in our opinion this is not the case for the new media technologies we are researching.

For this reason, we do not see our research as in the trajectory of discussions of post-human or cyborg studies that derived from the work of Haraway (1991) and others. These have been commonly linked to developments in digital worlds and new media. A recent example would be the volume edited by Whitehead and Wesch (2012) called *Human No More*. But discussions of topics such as memorialization, or changes in social networks through the advent of Facebook, that are contained in that volume seem to suggest quite the opposite. These are issues which are entirely encompassable within more traditional modes of anthropological enquiry into social change.

Finally, we need to prevent a theory of attainment being seen as merely *plus ça change*. We have suggested that our concept of attainment implies a kind of latency in the human condition, but not merely a litany of pre-given imagined abilities planted in evolutionary time and then coming into being with new technology. Technology is not some kind of kiss by a fairy tale prince that awakes another sleeping but beautiful exemplar of humanity. This latency is often something that itself is created with the advent of the most recent technology. There was no gene for writing that was frozen until the invention of the pen. Technology in and of itself transforms capacity and changes what human beings can do or can be envisaged as doing. The last of the four stages defined by Miller and Slater in examining technological change, which was called the expansive potential, concerns those aspirations that can only now be imagined thanks to these developments. Technology creates as well as realizes latency.

In the substantive chapters that follow, we give several examples of attainment that suggest webcam has allowed people to realize some ambition or latent function that had been envisaged but could only now be achieved. But there are an equal number of instances where it is highly unlikely that anyone had ever imagined or desired that which they were enabled to accomplish through webcam. It was the technology itself that stimulates new potentials or ideals. Chapter Three, in dealing with intimacy, describes an entirely unprecedented series of media configurations, what we call 'always-on', which leads to new imaginations of how people could 'live' together, while still in entirely separate places. The point we are making is that being human is not something that should be reduced to our past, or even our present, but something that must include also our future. The reason we need a theory of attainment is because we need to acknowledge that something that will be invented ten centuries from now, which we cannot even begin to imagine, will still be part of our humanity, because most probably (though not necessarily) we will still be human.

Webcam and attainment

How do the ideas discussed in this conclusion, and most especially the theory of attainment, derive from an ethnographic study of the use of webcam? How in turn does our contextualization in ethnography help to neutralize the moral connotations of a word such as 'attain'? The next chapter concerns the topic of self-consciousness. It starts from the observation that when people use webcam though Skype and other facilities, they become intensely aware of the small box in one corner of the screen in which they see themselves. The reason for this, it is suggested, is that although in the past we have had mirrors, photographs or videos, in all such cases, we strike poses or in some ways perform the image that we then see. By contrast, when we are on Skype for an hour's conversation, we cannot maintain these conscious performances for any great length of time. As a result, and for the very first time in human history, we routinely observe ourselves as we have appeared to others in the course of ordinary conversation.

How does this illustrate a theory of attainment? As soon as we consider in abstraction the potential capacity of a human being to see themselves as others see them, we can quickly appreciate how absurd it would be to assume that an inability to see ourselves as others see us is somehow the natural condition of humanity. It is only the past condition of humanity. Such a natural condition exists mainly in myth. The Greek myth of Narcissus implies a phase in the human condition prior to knowing our own appearance until perchance a man spies himself in the surface of a lake, with in that case rather dire consequences. That was the birth of self-consciousness. The psychoanalyst Lacan (2001) could be considered an equivalent myth maker. Piaget's (1999) constructivism is a better guide than Lacan. Even as children, we are the ones that construct this capacity for concern as to how we appear to others. Anthropologists insist that this is cultural. We dwell within a huge city of structures of embarrassment and shame, makeovers, self-consciousness and embellishments of personal appearance. There are many people today who refuse to have their photograph taken lest it steals their soul (Behrend, 2003; Hoskins, 2009). Yet, it was always the case that people might have, for all sorts of reasons, wanted to know how they looked to others in routinized everyday conversational mode, and even without webcam, we took considerable measures to construct what we hoped was the best or an acceptable version of this imagined self. Recent archaeological discoveries of cosmetic pigments in sites inhabited by Neanderthals suggest these structures have foundations even earlier than our modern species. We have always possessed the cultural desire to see ourselves as others see us. What has been lacking is the technology. So webcam is not some artificial transformation of what it is to be culturally human. It is more a bringing of machines-as-technology up to scratch with culture-as-technology. Though, as Chapter Two demonstrates, this has now been supplemented by the desire of most users to also 'put on a face' for the express purpose of appearing on webcam.

The subsequent chapters make similar and analogous points with respect to other aspects of life that are exposed through the advent of webcam. Chapter Three addresses the topic of intimacy, where the case for a theory of attainment is perhaps even stronger. The very term 'intimacy' carries with it the connotations of the most unmediated and most natural aspect of our relationships. Whether this pertains to the essential and physical co-presence of two people engaged in sexual intercourse or the immediacy involved in the intense and emotional experience of parenting, we assume we know what ought to be considered intimate. Webcam seems, at first, to be precisely an artificial mediation that creates an improper, denuded and, quite possibly, fake version of intimacy. But as this chapter unfolds, we see a very different story.

What we come to realize is the degree to which, prior to webcam, all forms of intimacy were thoroughly dependent upon the construction of particular conditions of ambience that allowed people to have these feeling of togetherness. Because of webcam, we come to appreciate just how much work it had taken to create the conditions of feeling natural and close. This is perhaps clearest in the discussion of what we call 'always-on' webcam, which attempts to construct the intimacy of the 'natural' co-presence of two people living together in the same house and sharing the same rooms. Exactly as befits a digital anthropology, it is only with the advent of webcam that we come to appreciate the quite bizarre nature of living together under the same roof with all its subtle rules of speech and silence, attendance and aversion. Once again, using webcam is a bit like reading Goffman; it shows us how we had failed to appreciate, failed even to see how much the everyday life of people living under the same roof depended upon complex mediations. Similarly, it is webcam that helps confirm the centrality, indeed dependency, of co-present sex upon fantasy, and why in some cases people need webcam to repair the damage of co-present sexual relations and come back to a relationship to sex itself that is sustainable and feels comfortable. As a result, this chapter provides several original insights as to what intimacy, and also sex, has previously been, but which had been hidden under the leaden opacity of the terms natural and authentic.

Chapter Four reiterates these points with respect to our sense of place or location and particularly the idea of home. Building on the previous discussion of co-presence, does being together actually mean paying attention to each other? Often during a divorce it is argued that it did not. This discrepancy is clarified by the advent of webcam, because webcam foregrounds the question of whether or not another person is actually giving you their attention. This is just one of several ways the chapter shows how webcam destabilizes and problematizes the notion of home, but then in turn reconstructs a concept and experience of home in its own right. There is a new kind of home that is found through another kind of co-presence within Dr Who's 'Tardis' of the computer – so small on the outside, so capacious within. The computer is now a place within which people live. Here, attainment reflects on transformations that we probably didn't envisage until webcam sparked a further imagination of how we could be. But as so often in this book, this radicalism in imagination does not derive from any sort of futurism. The pioneers are not geeks, the discovery of how to live together online is more often a result of the anguish of a couple deeply in love, but separated by distance.

Such concerns lead naturally to a focus upon relationships in Chapter Five. We begin with formulating a theory of retainment, as well as attainment, as the use of webcam becomes inseparable from these issues of separation. For this purpose, we need to define what we mean by a relationship. Relationships such as between parents and children, or between siblings, contain considerable tensions, as they incorporate both powerful ideals of what such relationships should be like, and the knowledge of the discrepancies between these ideals and what they are actually like. We show how webcam may accentuate these contradictions but also, in certain instances, help to resolve them. What may be attained is an ability for parents and children to achieve something closer to their ideal balance between autonomy and support, partly due to webcam. What may be attained can equally be an exacerbated failure that exposes all that is wrong in a relationship.

By Chapter Six it should be evident that we cannot fully appreciate webcam if we treat it in isolation. If we are becoming more conscious of how our relationships are mediated, this is obviously not through an isolated experience of webcam. Webcam arose alongside developments in half a dozen other new media, not one of which seems capable of sitting still. The pack of Facebook, smartphones and others are restless beasts and this dynamism lies not merely within each object but also in respect to their changing relationship to each other. Texting exists as a technology in its own right, but it may also be how you check whether someone is ready to see you on Skype. By thereby making webcam less obtrusive, texting may also make webcam more acceptable.

Understanding each media in the context of all the others is what we call 'polymedia'. But, polymedia turns out be much more than merely the configuration of disparate media into a package of familiar usage. We show that as issues of cost and access recede into the background, polymedia becomes a kind of re-socializing of communications. The decision to use this media when you might have used that one has become something a person will be judged for. So polymedia uncovers the moral aspect of choosing between media. This in turn helps us to explore topics such as the conveying and controlling of emotions across different media, and the place of power in communication within relationships.

Finally, in Chapter Seven, we turn to the single property that is foundational to most people's use of webcam, which is visibility in itself. We use this chapter to broaden from examples taken from personal communication and use evidence largely derived from our studies of webcam usage within commercial contexts. We examine criteria such as functionality and the pragmatic, which dominate the legitimation of webcam used within commerce. This investigation shows how much is at stake in achieving visibility. As Barthes (1977) demonstrated with respect to photography, the element of communication that seems to be at the heart of the visual image is the issue of truth and veracity. This derives in part from webcam's prior association more generally with surveillance. We show how both within and outside commerce these come together, as veracity becomes closely linked to issues of trust.

Webcam is utilized, just as photography was before it, as a kind of meta-symbol for truth itself, so that people feel the need to attest to the visual even if there are no good grounds for thinking this is actually more truthful as a medium. This creates an argument that webcam is dialectically a simultaneous increase in what people regard as truth and also as falsehood. By focusing upon business practice, we can see how this becomes grounded in the everyday work of transactional communications. Passing from there to issues of truth and trust within personal relationships, this returns us to questions of moral truth and visibility as the acknowledgment of the basic humanity of another person, which in turn brings us back to the issues of self-consciousness, intimacy and presence as explored in the early chapters. By this stage, we hope that our theory of attainment has itself attained the status we aspired for. The intention is to remove it from issues of judgement, or approaches to new media that imply a growth or diminishing of our humanity. Instead, we see how the study of new media becomes a tool for conventional anthropology, helping us to better appreciate the capacity that was always there within culture for mediating and thereby constituting human communication and relationships.

A note on method and context

The material that informed this book is derived from a number of different sources. Although we view this as, in essence, an ethnographic work, the bedrock, in terms of material that has been used extensively in writing the book, is probably a core of some seventy interviews that were carried out in Trinidad between November 2011 and March 2012, while Sinanan was living in the small town of El Mirador. Some of these were conducted jointly (Miller joined Sinanan for December), while more were carried out by Sinanan alone. Sinanan has also been able to build upon her kinship connections, especially her extensive set of cousins (her father is Trinidadian with five siblings who had children) and friendships. These connections go back many years and had naturally included her own participation in webcamming between Australia, where she was brought up, and these Trinidadians. These experiences predated any plan to research webcam. As such, they already revealed how webcam could facilitate a re-connecting with one's own kin, which in turn had become the reason Sinanan formed the desire to carry out fieldwork in Trinidad. While in Trinidad, Sinanan also webcammed with her family and friends in Australia and London, which in turn contributed to the comparative aspect of ethnographic study. On returning home, she continued to webcam with Trinidadians in El Mirador. In these periods, she also accumulated twenty hours of recorded webcam sessions. Although it is true that we have both participated in active webcamming, including webcam experience with Trinidadians and some of those in Miller's pilot study, it is not easy to actually observe people in the act of webcamming and expect them to act normally, as this can seem quite artificial, so we would not particularly privilege that aspect of fieldwork.

Miller had previously carried out a pilot study, specifically on the use of webcam, that included sixteen interviews at UCL, and these often figure in the subsequent text, because they give breadth to what otherwise would be entirely a Trinidad-based work. We have several discussions about specifically Trinidadian cultural genres, but these are highlighted partly by having a number of our examples and stories taken from people who are not Trinidadian. These were mainly students, mostly from other countries such as Brazil, individuals most of whom Miller had known reasonably well for several years. There is also material derived from Miller's prior research on Facebook and transnational families in Trinidad carried out with Mirca Madianou in 2010 (Miller, 2011; Madianou and Miller, 2012a). For Miller, this is his fifth book based on fieldwork in Trinidad, and other informants in this study are people he has known for decades, long before webcam existed. Again, there is a broader context of knowledge than just the interviews. This is one of the reasons that this book has perhaps an unfortunate propensity to cite Miller. This is also a result of the book being jointly authored, but more because the ideas discussed reflect a long trajectory of prior development in Miller's research in Trinidad, including his previous four ethnographic books on Trinidad (Miller, 1994, 1997, 2011, Miller and Slater, 2000). We are uncomfortable with this, but did not find a way to avoid such self-citation without thereby eliminating essential background materials and an acknowledgment of the trajectory of these ideas.

There has been a tradition within anthropology of playing down the role of the interview in favour of a sometimes quite strident conception of participant observation. We believe that this work has benefited from a mix of resources and data collection. We have no desire to repudiate or limit our acknowledgement of the role of the interview, which has been central to our understanding of webcam. At one time, the recorded interview was almost frowned upon as secondary to hanging out and participation for anthropologists, but in a recent book edited by Skinner

(2012), many leading anthropologists have acknowledged that the interview can take centre stage within ethnographic research, without this being thereby viewed as a vulgar or impoverished form of research. Skinner gives a more considered discussion of the merits, limitations and specificity of the interview within wider anthropological enquiry.

Such an acknowledgement is just as well, in that anthropologists increasingly work in places such as the UK, where the more traditional forms of participant observation become implausible, simply because the nodes of sociality they depend upon are so attenuated. One could spend all one's time in a pub, but that would only really be an anthropology of pubs, not of the English. Hockey (2002), working largely in the UK, shows just why ethnography should not be reduced solely to participant observation and can include a greater appreciation of the interview, in an increasingly private world where hanging out extensively in the private home may not be an option. One advantage of this core of interviews is that we have made considerable use of direct quotation in our account.

If there remain issues with describing this work as ethnographic, they should be still further diminished by the expansion of the wider ethnographic encounter, which was based exclusively on participant observation. This additional fieldwork came about when Sinanan returned to the same field site from November 2012 through to April 2013, accompanied by Miller from December 2012 through to February 2013. In total, Sinanan has had ten months of participatory ethnographic fieldwork in addition to her long-term contacts that preceded the ethnography. This second stay in Trinidad was also the occasion for our joint completion of this manuscript, carried out while living in the town of the study itself. Usually, ethnographies are written at a distance from the field, but, in this case, having the writing of the book coincide with renewed joint fieldwork in our study site has been immensely valuable in helping us to reflect further on our findings and conclusions.

Because this book is based on a variety of sources, with both of us having contacts elsewhere in Trinidad and including material from the UK, we do not see this as an ethnography of El Mirador, though that was the main site of fieldwork. We are conscious that we frequently use the term 'Trinidadians' (or 'Trinis') while being perfectly aware that that is not a statement that would be true of every person in the island, but crave indulgence for the necessity of such generalizations in social science. Since completing the fieldwork for this volume, we have begun a long-term research project where the focus is more similar to the traditional anthropological monograph, in that it is very much an ethnography of the town of El Mirador. It will form part of a seven-country comparison within the 'Global Social Media Impact Study' (www.gsmis.org). This is why we are in El Mirador writing this manuscript. The emphasis in this future work will be on the impact of new social media in terms of the sociality of the town itself. For the purpose of the present volume, it should be sufficient to note that El Mirador is a small rural town in Trinidad. The population is around 25,000, depending on where you draw the boundaries. It is a hub for the villages in the area, but sufficiently far from any larger settlement as to be seen as something of a backwater. The population is fairly typical of Trinidad in that we would estimate that the demography reflects national figures of around 40 per cent ex-African slave descent, 40 per cent ex-South Asian indentured labour descent, with the rest being mixed and otherwise from all over the place. It lies in one of the poorest regions of Trinidad and is generally regarded by Trinidadians as a quiet town of no particular interest, a place people come from and otherwise merely pass through. Yet, El Mirador is also a town that is seen as retaining traditional Trinidadian values of community and family orientation.

2

Self-Consciousness

One might have expected this book to start with the way relationships are constituted and maintained by webcam as a form of communication. Yet, about a third of the way through our fieldwork, we started to appreciate that there was an unpredicted, but possibly quite profound observation that might also arise from our material. There was at least one sense in which communicating through webcam could be described as the very first time that human beings have been able to see who they are. The argument would have gone as follows: of course people have been able to see themselves in mirrors and, more recently, through photography. But, as when caught on video, these tended to be relatively self-conscious appearances that are often created for that performance. There is, however, a good reason why so many people who use Skype become drawn, after a while, from the person who occupies most of the screen to the small box nestled often in one corner, within which they are confronted by an animated vision of themselves. The self that they are drawn to is one they have never seen before. This is not the self as portrayed to the self. It is the way they look to those others with whom they engage in regular conversation, as speaker or audience. Given the extended period of time involved, after a while, people relax from the more controlled and self-conscious performance of themselves, into the more routine gestures and responses that have become an unconscious and naturalized self – the one others have long known, but that sometimes is a revelation to themselves. After half an hour they have returned to the person they would usually have been in the kinds of conversations where they used not to be able to see themselves. Yet, this person they now encounter is in many ways the one they have always been most concerned and anxious about. Not the subjective *I*, but, for all those other people, the apparently objective *you*. This is the person whom other people meant when they use the word 'you' in reference to them.

They have never previously been fully aware of this more sustained presentation of themselves to others, the self from which they may well garner their idea of their personality and nature. For *I* as *me* to suddenly encounter the *I* as *you* is likely to be a striking and potentially disconcerting revelation. There will almost inevitably be some aspects of that appearance which are unexpected or different from the previous imagination the viewer had had of how they appear to others. The way they come across as animated or reticent, the quirks and gestures that they repeat or that punctuate their discussion, their listening pose and detailed landscape of eyes, lips and face may, in some degree, differ from what they had always imagined. Even if there are no such discrepancies and this is merely an affirmation of their expectations, they are likely to have a heightened consciousness of themselves as occupying the gaze of others.

To speak of self-consciousness implicates some concept of the self. Anthropologists argue that there are many versions of the self. We will illustrate this with the case most relevant to the material we are about to explore. Miller (1994) has previously argued that there is a fundamental difference between the Trinidadian understanding of the location of being and that held by populations such as the English. The English subscribe to what he called a 'depth ontology'; a belief that the reality or truth of the person lies deep within, and the surface is superficial. A profound person is deep, while those interested in mere appearances are shallow. Miller argued that Trinidadians, by contrast, have the opposite view of ontology. For them, deep inside the person is where we keep secrets and lies, while the truth of that person is evident on the surface and subject to the judgement and view of others, who can directly attest to what they have seen. With regard to appearance, the 'truth' comes from an ability to create a look and a style, against which we can be judged. In England people sometimes suggest that putting on cosmetics is an artificial masking of the true or natural self. The Trinidadian view is the opposite. A person might be born with brown hair and freckles. While that may be natural, it should not be used as evidence for the self, because they did not create it. The self is found in what a person does to create themselves. This argument builds upon that of other anthropologists. Strathern (1979), working in highland New Guinea, argued in a paper called 'The self in self-decoration' that more hierarchical societies tend to believe in this deeper internal self that can be institutionalized and retained as a longer term project. The self is a farmer, an aristocrat or has a PhD. Egalitarian societies, on the other hand, are more likely, as in Trinidad, to see the self on the surface as open to the judgement of others. This makes 'the self' more transient, because unlike the institutionalized self, which is created by the outside, for example, judgement as to your class position, Trinidadians see the self as created by the inside, which is then externalized for the judgement of others. The implication of this would be that the ability to see oneself as others see you would have a quite different consequence for a Trinidadian than for someone from England.

At this point, such philosophical and anthropological generalities need to be grounded. What is the evidence we are trying to account for? To begin, we introduce a young male Trinidadian for whom this advent of self-consciousness does indeed seem to matter a great deal.

Colin

The evidence that Colin has quite an extreme concern with how he himself looks during a webcam session, extreme even within a Trinidadian context, is that he is almost the only case we know of a person who regularly uses two screens. He does this so that in shifting his glance between them, he gains a clear view of how he looks to the person he is speaking with. This began when he became aware of the discrepancy between where a person is actually looking and where they appear to be looking during a webcam session. To seem to be looking at a person means making eye contact with the webcam, not their eyes on the screen. One result of this is that his degree of self-absorption had become evident to others and a source of annoyance to them. One friend told him, 'The only reason you want to talk to me is because you want to look at yourself!' Colin claims this is true, and not just of him. He has three cats, two dogs and a parrot, and the cats in particular have a habit of wanting to be at the centre of attention, so they will often come and sit on the keyboard between the correspondents.

At first, Colin talks about his naturalness in front of the webcam. He is simply so relaxed at home that he doesn't even need to wear a shirt. It's not an activity for which he feels the need to be concerned about his appearance at all. In fact, he tells us, if it was up to him, he would be lying in bed with his laptop on his stomach, and the main reason he doesn't do this is because the laptop itself gets far too hot, and in the tropics, people are too hot already. Maybe, he speculates, in a cool climate it could double as a sort of hot water bottle/communication device.

But after a while, you realize that the reason he has no shirt on is not at all a sign of how relaxed he is. It's actually so he can show off his highly toned body.

> Yes, I play sports and go to the gym, so if I'm on the camera, sometimes shirtless, I'll twist my arm and ask 'ay how ah looking now?' Sometimes it's incidental, so sometimes I'll be watching it and I'll be like 'ay, my hair looks good this way.' Sometimes the person will be talking and I'll be like 'Wait nah, I looking real good there.' And I won't even take on what they're saying and then I'll be like 'Sorry wat yuh was sayin again, because I really wasn't taking you on jus now, you have to say that again' I mean you know what they say if yuh can't love yourself, yuh can't love anybody else. I tend to get distracted a lot and I'm a Taurus so I'm very vain.

Colin has a whole litany of similarly self-conscious modes of performance – 'Sometimes I tend to lean in to the computer, like this [leans forward] or the majority of the time when I'm explaining stuff, I tend to lean back. If I'm arguing, I won't be shouting, I'll just be disagreeing, I'm very serious and I will just sit down and my hands are still and on my chin like this [motions with one hand on chin and the other at his elbow] but when I'm trying to get the point across, I'll be like this [motions with hands].' It's not only these forms of performed expression; he also understands that, at least for a Trini, much depends on setting the atmosphere, which always means getting the right music on in the background. So he will preselect the sound that sets the frame and tone for the conversation he expects to be having, and he sees this as a common thing for Trinidadians to do. With a friend who was abroad and missing the Christmas season, he knew that having Christmas parang music (a type of 'Spanish' folk music with Venezuelan and Amerindian heritage, usually played at Christmas time) on in the background would be much appreciated as a kind of extra gift within the wider communication.

Colin has no problem therefore with female friends who will delay putting on the camera until they have done their face, their hair and whatever else that makes them feel comfortable. In fact, it is often they who complain when he appears online insufficiently dressed as far as they are concerned. Colin in his own right constructs an account of what he is doing that seems to readily affirm the argument just made that what is being performed to others is seen not as artifice but the truth of a person, the way they discover who they are. Now that webcam exists, Colin feels it makes no sense to be speaking to someone without you being able to look at them and they look at you. He simply doesn't understand why some people would persist in not turning on their webcam. More so, he thinks he does understand, and that's why he is so insistent upon having webcam on. The problem is that of the two friends living abroad he most regularly Skypes with, one has a habit of also being in conversation with others at the same time, and this only becomes obvious when the webcam is on, which is why they are reluctant to use it. This merely confirms for Colin that if someone isn't automatically adding the visual to their conversation, there is probably something they are trying to hide. As he puts it, 'But I get kinda short tempered because I'll be like "I'm speaking to you, you have to give me full attention so I would like you to put on yuh camera." But sometimes it doesn't work out so I'll be like arite, well laterz, whateva, I doh wanna talk to you.' In short, he will no longer put up with the lie that for him is constituted by a conversation without webcam.

These observations relate not only to visual appearance, but also to the content and style of conversation itself. One of the most significant early anthropological works on the Caribbean was called *The Man-of-Words in the West Indies* by Roger Abrahams (1983), and it concerned the performative nature of talk.

It's both what you say and how you say it. One of the favourite modes of conversation in Trinidad goes beyond the banter of many regions to become a sort of competitive insult. This is now more globally familiar from rap contests such as those portrayed in Eminem's film *8 Mile*. When Miller was first working in Trinidad, people still used traditional terms such as '*picong*' or giving '*fatigue*' for this genre, but by 2011, young people referred to this as 'shit-talk'. Competitive shit-talk is fast and funny and uses so much local dialect that most non-Trinis cannot follow it. In the same way that Fox (2004) in her book *Watching the English* analyses the place of certain light banter in the English pub, shit-talk is the essence of that wider sociality of '*liming*' or hanging around. Shit-talk is not just language; it is a performance and involves a litany of gesturing, which is another reason Colin feels it makes no sense at all to try to talk to someone when you can't see them. What keeps shit-talk from being aggressive is the humour and you need to see the laughter in the response, and the gestures that tell you the insult is a game, nothing personal.

In a way, Colin has understood that webcam manages to overcome what previously had been a real limitation in all prior forms of communication. Until now, when involved in shit-talk, all you could do was see the person you were communicating with. But given the nature of this competitive performance, it is much better if you can see yourself and monitor how well you are doing; not just be able to see the other person you are exchanging such banter with. This is not something you can do in face-to-face conversation, because you are invisible to yourself. It is only now, when webcam exists, that we have a technology which has caught up with how the practice should always have been. As in the theory of attainment, shit-talk on webcam has finally become what it always should have been. So Colin simply doesn't understand it when other people suggest online webcam communication is less real. On the contrary, it's only with online webcam that people finally get to be able to talk as one really should. The reason this matters is that Colin engages in this kind of shit-talk with his friends in London and New Orleans as well as with those around him in Trinidad, almost every single day.

Because Colin understands conversation as performance, he also sees his own conversation as framed by clear and separated out genres. Just as in theatre, where there is tragedy and comedy, for him there is shit-talk, but there is also the formal conversation he has with one particular relative. Whereas shit-talk is in dialect, this is based on more formal English. This genre of 'serious' talk is used in conversation with the individual with whom he most often webcams, because she is living abroad and is constantly wanting to discuss with him the problems she is having with her boyfriend. For him, that involves a shift from his normal demeanour, where he is always smiling, to a far more sombre visage. Another advantage of webcam is that this framing of the conversation which sets the tone is obvious to his interlocutor. They can see his deference to the topic of discussion. Controlled and appropriate self-expression is much more awkward with text, where he will type the words 'I'm very serious right now', in order to set the appropriate frame for what follows. Some of this genre creation is specific to an individual. He has one friend for whom it is clear you must never interrupt them; they need to get the whole story out, and only then is it okay to make some intervention. For them, everything is done properly in turns.

These issues surrounding the control over the frame of the interaction become even more obvious when one or the other gets angry. In the case of his New Orleans friend, Colin uses webcam as a mode of authority. When she starts losing control of herself, he simply turns off the webcam so that he can't see what by then have become her fairly wild gestures. She gets mad at this, but also comes to appreciate that there is not much point becoming so expressive when he can no longer see her. This gesture makes it an effective means for achieving a return to what he sees as a more useful and relaxed exchange. Of course, 'if she's really really mad, she stops the call altogether. I would wait and she would call back. The next time we talk, it'll be normal, I'll be like, "So you wanna talk now?"' This systematic manipulation of the webcam as a frame to conversation can be even more contrived. Colin has noted that Skype, and other online devices, provide background information as to whether you are actually online or not. This may seem a straightforward device, but, as Colin notes, it very quickly became appropriated as an aspect of Trinidadian *bacchanal* (a term which will be more fully explained below). He gives an extended description of a woman who has become *vexed* (angry) with her boyfriend. What she will do is manipulate Skype so that she appears as offline to him. She does this at a time and in a manner such that he knows that she is online and she is just adopting this offline pose as a negative gesture to him alone. The little green and red lights of online presence and absence become another weapon in the endless negotiation of relationships across the sexes.

Colin exemplifies aspects of the theory of attainment introduced in the previous chapter. At any given time, a population is often aware of what they see as the limitations of the status quo – the way things have always been done. Life is often experienced as frustration. When a new technology appears, they are not at first looking for some entirely new potential in that technology. Rather, they seize upon the technical ability to resolve what was experienced as an infuriating lack within previous communications; something they should always have been able to do but technically couldn't. For Colin, people should always have been able to have had one eye upon themselves while engaged in conversation with others. That would always have been far more natural; it simply wasn't previously possible. This is why the fact that Colin employs two distinct screens, so that he can glance across monitors and gain a better idea of how he looks to the other, no longer seems quite so weird and strange. Instead, it could be testimony to the degree to which Colin follows through a logic, at least to Trinidadian modes of self-consciousness, that most people were less aware of. This may be partly because it didn't matter quite so much to them as to Colin. It may also be because most people are simply not as quick as Colin in moving themselves from the comforting embrace of the conventional and taken-for-granted in communicative acts.

Colin is the first of our extended examples and raises a question. He certainly seems quite extreme concerning his self-regard. This is part of the reason he appears at this point. But in other respects, the evidence points clearly to cultural generalities that apply to him and many of our subsequent cases. Should we treat him largely as a particular individual, or as an example to be used for anthropological generalizations about Trinidad, or a psychological argument pertaining to humanity as a whole? As it happens, the one book by an anthropologist with the very title *Self-Consciousness* by Cohen (1994) is a treatise against the subsuming of individuals, such as Colin, within more conventional analytical generalization. Cohen and, more recently, Rapport (1997) have tried to establish an alternative anthropological tradition that is focused more on the capacity of individuals to be more than merely the consequences of social and cultural context. We hope that we respect the points made by Cohen and Rapport by including such extended cases, which are intended to acknowledge the humanism of individual difference and delight in the creative inventiveness of individuality.

On the other hand, the main original insights to be gained from the case of Colin, and our subsequent examples, are obtained through the conventions of anthropological generalization. Take the discussion of shit-talk. This cannot be just about Colin. There cannot be individual language. Shit-talk is an entirely characteristic genre of Trinidad with similarities to connected traditions within other populations that may derive from older African lineages, as suggested by the similarity to rap in Black America (Gates, 1990). It therefore seems entirely justifiable to understand at least some of this account as part of a comparative perspective on self-consciousness, emphasizing the difference between Trinidadians in general and others in general. It would seem that Colin is clearly performing himself in order to control how he is seen by others. This is not evidence that this self is untrue or unreal, because it follows from the Trinidadian concept of ontology. As such, Colin would be quite similar to the character Vishala, who appears in Miller's (2011) book *Tales from Facebook*. Vishala provides six further arguments as to why the self that appears on Facebook, as constructed, is a truer image of the self than the one you might meet in the flesh.

If the state of being for Trinidadians is something that pertains to the outside of the person which others can attest to, then webcam might be seen as a more truthful form of communication for them, precisely because they can now see themselves as others see them, which is tantamount to who they truly are. This would not be the case, at least not to the same degree, for the English. Colin is the start; other examples will arise during the subsequent chapters, which cumulatively reinforce our view that in order to understand webcam we must appreciate that it will have quite different meanings and consequences for different populations.

Here, we have the level of individual creativity, and that of anthropological generality. But, we also cannot ignore that most people today use the term self-consciousness in a more general manner derived from common discussion on TV and in newspapers and which connotes a more general and psychological level. At the other end of the scale, the introduction to this chapter discussed the meaning of self-consciousness per se. Some elements that emerge from our account of Colin are neither peculiar to Trinidad, nor indeed to webcam. Consider this discussion of *Madam Bovary* by Melchior-Bonnet in her history of the mirror: 'Emma, dreaming of Paris, imagines the capital as a salon decorated with mirrors in which ambassadors flit around. She constantly interrupts her gestures in order to look at herself in the mirror . . . The reflection reinforces her determination to escape her mediocre reality and challenges her to maintain her fictive self, more beautiful than reality' (2002: 182). At least for Flaubert (1996), the idea of switching between two screens was already a possibility. Most people have probably used mirrors in that manner at some time or other.

Self-consciousness and embarrassment

The first and most obvious form of self-consciousness, when faced with the small box in which people see themselves on Skype, is simply the same kind of embarrassment or concern an individual might experience in any public arena. For example, a 17-year-old Trini male notes, 'I get very self conscious because I see this little screen on the side of me and I'm like "Oh my God! Look at me, I need to lose weight, look at my hair, it's greasy" everything, I go mad, I seriously go mad, and so what I do is I try to focus on my grandmother, and I speak to her and I try to forget on the side that there's a little box on me.' A Trini woman notes, 'Yeah um . . . I think that talking on the internet is sort of unflattering because, especially if you're doing it in a room without other lights on, cause then it's just that blaring light from the computer screen that's staring at you in the face, and then I know I've definitely gone and put a hat on after having a crazy hair day, or things like that, definitely.' Another says, 'Sometimes I actually talk with my hands on my head because I don't want to show my hair loss.' Even when looking at the other person, this is such a close-up encounter that it rebounds back onto self-consciousness, as in 'I am looking at them and how they look as well as what they say, and how is their hair or whatever. And then I'm looking at myself. I look terrible, I didn't put on any makeup, I look really tired, and I'm wearing glasses, whatever.'

These fears exacerbate prior anxieties: 'Oh God, well it hits a fearful point, even when I choose a photo for an online dating thing, I don't think I'm that photogenic, and so the image that is put up even on that is partial . . . Because you're sort of watching them watch you, and you're also aware of what you look like in that same instance.' Many people would suggest that the situation is worse on webcam than face-to-face, precisely because you also see yourself: 'I think, I think the level of self consciousness might be more on Skype, because I'm seeing what they're seeing. As opposed to I have a mental picture here, I have an actual picture there. Your mental picture's always telling you to be nice, but your actual picture is showing otherwise. And you also tend to remember the nice things, not the bad things, depending on how you are. You might be, you know, your ears too big and your eyes too small. So you tend to be a little more conscious on Skype.'

Others who are more self-confident about their appearance, report this heightened self-consciousness when they first engage with webcam, but suggest that this may quickly disappear as the media becomes familiar and routine. Indeed, they may even welcome the fact that webcam, just like Flaubert's Emma, with her mirror, can keep them up to date with how they appear to the other: 'Yes, I always leave that little window so I can see myself, so I'm like constantly, if my hair is out of place, I would just fix it.' In this case, being able to see an image of herself reinforces her self-confidence. Others may use the option of simply removing that small box in which they appear, or, as in this case, gradually come to accept it as they get used to its presence:

> Initially, I would say I have it up because I like myself, or I don't have it up because I don't like how I'm looking. But now, it doesn't really matter. I think I may tend to have it up, because it stays up when it comes up, I don't close it off. I've gotten used to it. Initially I was ehh that's how I looking – that's what they see! Of course as you get older you get less conscious of yourself and how you're looking, I mean the physical perspective. So that could be the reason you're more comfortable with it, cos you get more comfortable with yourself.

These concerns may be general or specific to the person with whom one is interacting. For example, Sassatelli (2010) describes what she calls mirror-work. She describes the way women in Milan check their appearance very carefully in actual mirrors, making sure the fit of their blue jeans also makes them look 'fit' in the sense of sexually attractive, and the bedrock this provides for self-confidence when going into situations where they might encounter attractive males. A Trini woman notes, 'Well actually I would put on my makeup and stuff before I use it, especially if I was talking to a guy. I would freshen up my face and make sure my hair was well properly combed. I know it's silly, but if it's my aunt or my mom, yeah they could see me, I wouldn't mind.' Another notes, 'I won't ever webcam with my friends when I am about to go to bed and I'm in my pyjamas without any makeup on.' The point being that this is something she would never have done outside of webcam.

Since webcam is dominated by very close relationships such as sisters or partners, many people say they simply would not care how they looked. A 30-year-old Trini woman states, 'Yeah and I'm not going to try to change it, so I'm not going to try to pull back my hair, try to pass a brush through it, try to pinch the cheeks to make them look alive, no no no. Exactly as you see me is how you take me.' Sometimes, however, the media can get in the way of the image the partners would like them to create. A woman says she can tell her partner wants her to look 'hot' and he thinks she does. But as far as she is concerned, 'When you're in your bed you're like this, and you get all that fat there (around her neck), you know? I'm telling you, you're not hot when you're lying there like this, cause it's 11 pm, and I'm exhausted. I'm in my bed, I'm ready for bed, it's really not "hot".' Another problem with webcam may be that a person is happy to feel natural and relaxed in front of their best friend or partner, but then another person may wander into a position where they can be seen. This is contrasted with offline, where people are more likely to knock on the door and respect their privacy. The intrusion seen on the screen can be a shock. 'When I was speaking to one of them and one of her friends, a guy came in and I was in a mess, in my pyjamas, my hair was messy and I was like "no you don't do that" and I just ran away.' On another occasion the situation was reversed, as she wandered into the room and became witness to the kind of quarrel that might have abated offline. But the participants being on webcam seemed oblivious to her and this became embarrassing.

As well as self-consciousness being relative to the person one is talking to, it is also relative to the place they are in. Often, Trinidadian parents who are concerned with security insist that computers are situated in the public space where they can oversee the communications their children are involved in. As a result, young people had to strike a balance between acknowledging their parents' concerns for their computer usage, which they largely shared, and being able to have a private conversation through webcam. Teenagers in Trinidad, like elsewhere, were likely to spend a lot of time in their rooms. By contrast, when it came to using laptops or computers, which are often in the public domain, they didn't quarrel or demand privacy from their parents. This may reflect the social organization of the family, where siblings often share their bedrooms through to early adulthood. As a result, young people would often use headphones or to type in the chat box. Similarly, Staci, who shares a student apartment with her university friend, tends not to be too concerned that her personal conversations might be overheard but is actually concerned not to use obscene language or sound offensive.

Being at home is defined as relaxed and informal, where one has taken off the clothes, and perhaps the makeup, of more formal encounters. This is more likely to equate to Goffman's (1959) backstage area of informality. People say they can't be bothered to put on a special face or look, just to go online. The trouble is, sometimes, the people they would not normally invite into the more intimate setting of the home, and who would not normally be exposed to this more natural and less prepared self, are through webcam, for the first time, entering into this more domestic space. This may equate with their sense of the real 'me' as in 'I'm at home. I really don't care, yeah once I'm relaxed, I'm relaxed and actually that's me in general. I tend not to put on a show, what you see is exactly what you get.' By contrast, several people clearly get their room ready and not just themselves, for example, when they will be talking with their parents. Webcam seems to return them to those conditions of moral surveillance for tidiness they experienced as a child. Or, as the 17-year-old male Trini notes, 'Yeah so I try to clean up the surroundings because my grandmother is one to note "Oh it's dirty there, go and clean up, sweep up" yeah, that's how she is.'

Is this the real you?

The anxiety and embarrassment about how one appears to others is common to most social encounters. And as people become familiar with this persona they are encountering online, they may also become equally concerned as to how far people see that image as a true representation of themselves, particularly when they are surprised by their online appearance. Most commonly, it is women who had a more idealized self-image and find their face is fatter or their profile isn't quite what they had hoped it to be. This would be the case for many of the quotations just given. For example, one woman said, 'When I first saw myself, I thought "Oh my God, do I really look like that all the time, my nose looks so flat. I was hoping I would look more the way I do in photos.' Another kind of discrepancy occurs when the self that appears on screen is experienced as a misleading representation of the person. For example,

> Interestingly, I have a tick, you know a tick, I twist my head or I move my eyes, I've been doing it ever since I was small, I don't know why, this is a nervous reaction, yes I know, when I'm nervous it comes on and sometimes even when I'm not nervous I still do it, and my dad has it as well. That as well for people who don't know me, you know, it might be looking on from the other side, they see me and you know, I don't know whether they, they never said anything, but you know it may make them uncomfortable, or you know they might be distracted by it, so I don't know, you know. But that's an interesting kind of element for people who have these kinds of tick.

Trinidadians will often draw the opposite conclusion and argue that online appearance attests to who they really are. They will talk about how they are a very straightforward kind of person, or that they are a typical introvert and point to their appearance on webcam as evidence for this. Webcam can also be exploited as an arena in which a person shows how they are true to themselves. For example, Margaret is a stay-at-home mother with three daughters, all under the age of five. She doesn't have a laptop at the moment, since her last one crashed, and she hasn't been able to repair or replace it. Margaret often visits a neighbour, who lets her Skype her friends with her laptop. Sometimes her daughters are there playing with the neighbour's children, and most of the time, she will carry on with the conversation. Margaret doesn't mind if the neighbour is in earshot; she is very close anyway. Margaret doesn't shy from confrontation, she's not afraid of a cuss-out, or standing her ground, and she respects people being up front with her as well.

> I'm a very straightforward person, so I would tell it as it is, maybe that is not easy for her, I don't take sides, I don't say sorry, I say what I have to say and that's it. There's right and there's wrong and that's it. I think I grew up like that. I would say, since I know myself, that is in me. Maybe too outspoken and that's a problem for some, but I'm a genuine person. Most people wouldn't like that, maybe they feel insecure about saying how things is, but I'm a genuine person, this is who I am, I cannot change that, I like being that way, I wouldn't like to be another way. So on webcam it's the same thing. As you see, when I talk, I talk with authority. That is who I am. If you are wrong or right, I would tell you if you're wrong or right, no BS [bullshit]. I'm not one to take sides, deal with it, whatever is the situation. If you look me in a way that you perceive me to be, but this is me . . . I find if you are this way home, when you're out you should be the same. Why should I feel like I am a saint when I'm out then when I am home I am a robot? No. The way I speak to my child at home, as you see here, that is how I speak to her. Anybody who would see me at home, I do the same thing. I don't have two faces. I cannot be like that. That double standard person, I cannot be, and I do not like double standard people. Who you are when you're in and out I'm the same. It's not like we're doing a flim or a show, you are who you are and that's it. [Trinis say flim rather than film]

So over webcam, Margaret expresses herself the way she would in person: she doesn't monitor or check herself; she will communicate in a visceral way, using her entire body, gesticulating and with facial expressions that express her internal feelings and her state of mind. Margaret thereby represents that same Trinidadian opposition to a depth ontology, seeing Skype more as an additional opportunity to attest to the truth of who she is through objectification. In that sense, webcam becomes something that, as it were, 'keeps you honest', revealing who you really are to yourself as much as to others.

Once again, this insight attests to more than the vagaries of an individual. It can also apply at the level of cultural normativity. Humphrey (2009) has argued, in a study of Russian chat rooms, that in using anonymity, Russians become emotional and expressive online; in a manner that they feel is closer to their true soul and real nature as Russians. They use all those expressive elements that they feel tend to be suppressed in ordinary offline conversations. In short, new media has helped make them conscious of their true self, not just as individuals, but also as Russians. As we have seen, Trinidadians tend not to look for hidden selves, but are concerned with the nature of the person who is being expressed to others.

This discussion of Margaret and the Russian soul brings out a rather different element to self-consciousness. It shows how for many people the concept of the self is as much to do with integrity in terms of their internal unity and consistency, as it is integrity in terms of truth. When someone talks of being straightforward, the point they are making is that their appearance is a representation of something much more general about them as a whole. They do not want appearance as it expresses them to others to differ from what they regard as the autobiographical narratives and continuities that Giddens (1991) identifies with a sense of the self. This desire for integrity is evident in the following example.

The Eye in Isis

It is extraordinary how some people have the ability to control how you see them. In the case of Isis from Chile, it is impossible to imagine that anyone can avoid starting with her eyes, and then her smile, and only then the rest of her. She consistently wears very bright eyeliner, often a different bright colour each day. This seems to capture the essence of a bright personality, but her smile does almost as good a job. This also means that she has, in a sense, pre-empted webcam. She already comes to each personal encounter as a face, through which you expect to see her personality in microcosm. As someone who had already featured her own eyes as the point of self-cultivation, it is not surprising that she confronts webcam as the capacity for eye-contact, which is vital to real conversation. 'But when you are looking at them, I think eye contact is very important, I like to look at people in the eye because it gives me a kind of feeling. I know if I can trust them. Basically because there are some conversations where it's not good to have just the [Microsoft] messenger . . . for example, when I had a special argument, when I argue with my husband by messenger, we said "ok now let's look at each other".'

Isis makes clear that this would be particularly true for the most important interactions, and then makes even clearer that the term important includes not just her husband but also her cats. The computer is placed on the floor and 'I start calling the cats "hey, come here, come see mommy", you know stupid things we say to cats, and they come yeah, and they start looking for me around the screen.' Of course, as any cat owner knows, it is precisely by narrowing the eyes that a cat acknowledges a close relationship with the person.

Isis feels that despite all her efforts, her eyes can betray her, as when her family tell her she shouldn't be studying all night, as seen from the fact that she has dark circles around her eyes. As it happens, she does often study all night and regards her face as a disaster area in the morning. So she has to spend time making herself up before she can countenance going on webcam. Even then, looking at the little box on the screen works better than any mirror in telling her what still needs to be done: 'Oh my nose looks horrible and I can see if I'm a bit fat in my cheeks and if my hair is ok, if I need a haircut.'

For the same reason, she is very aware of where exactly the point of eye contact is, and the fact that a person looking at their image on the screen doesn't actually then appear to be looking directly at them. At times, she will request her husband looks directly at the webcam instead, so that she can have the illusion of fully making eye contact. Not surprisingly, given the emphasis upon her own eyes, both her mother and her brother will frequently tell her to do the same thing, especially when they want to say how much they love her and miss her. It seems to require 'eye contact' even if that in turn can only be achieved by the deliberate refocus upon the camera. She appreciated how when a friend, and later on her parents, were telling her about the death of one of her cats, both must have spent the entire conversation staring at the webcam instead of the screen, because they had maintained the illusion that they were looking directly at her eyes. She says she had never realized this until we started talking about it.

Coming to England, she also realizes how much she associated eye contact with sincerity. She likes it when her professors look at her eyes when discussing her work, as a sign they are actually interested in both the work and her. This is especially important, as she lacks confidence in her English, and it is the eye contact that reassures her that they are following what she says. So, as was the case with Colin, the webcam is almost fortuitously a more truthful media, in as much as it allows a more deliberate focus upon the eyes. She is also aware of webcam's potential deceits. For example, sometimes, when she can't be bothered to talk to someone, her husband engages in the conversation while she carefully stays out of angle shot.

The relation to sincerity is particularly important in communicating with her husband, because the commitment to the visual aspect seems to convey the sense of care for each other, as making themselves present for each other. All their friends agree that they are a particularly close and loving couple, and we have witnessed the heartache when one or the other is alone in London. As with many couples, there may be a temporary shutting-off of the visual during a quarrel in order to make a point, which is not as problematic as shutting off the phone altogether. The visual is also useful because to disengage from the quarrel with her, her husband will sometimes imitate her appearance on webcam, which annoys her, but also makes her laugh, thereby ending the quarrelsome tone. He may also suddenly stop and ask her to 'do that again', i.e. pointing out her performative actions, and thereby implying that she is something of a drama queen on webcam.

She associates webcam with trust, truth and revelation. It may be the visual evidence that the person really cannot speak to you because they are busy or in the wrong place. Visual aids also show concern, as when he has especially tidied up the room or he is wearing the pyjamas she gave him. When her sister broke up a relationship, she wanted to appear strong and relatively unaffected, but she could only do this by resorting to text messaging and other short communications. Isis knew that once they were on webcam, and in eye contact, her sister would have to confront her actual sadness, and then they could talk truthfully about the situation.

Gradually, it emerges that this close correspondence between eye contact, sincerity and care for the other has made the experience of webcam instrumental in Isis' ability to construct her own philosophy of the self. When she was younger, she felt, like many young women, that she was unappealing, lacked good looks and thereby lacked self-confidence. 'I thought I was the ugliest girl in the school, I hated my hair. And I remember that I felt my eyes were too big and if I don't use any makeup, I look like a little ghost, very white, because my eyelashes are like that. So if I don't put some colour, I look too pale, so that's as far as I can see.' It was the self-affirmation that came with the transformation of her appearance through adopting bright eye-liner that was effective in her ability to create a sense of herself that in turn bolstered her self-esteem. This is reinforced today, when it is her students who ask her for makeup advice. The point was that her given 'natural' face, as pale, failed to correspond to what she saw as her bright lively personality. But with bright eyeliner, and the use of different colours, which could even correspond to different moods, she was able to create herself as she understood herself to be. Finally, her eyes could speak the truth of herself as a colourful person.

This became crucial to her marriage, which went okay for the first six months, but was not entirely satisfactory. Part of the problem was not her husband's behaviour, but her difficulty reconciling her status as married with her commitment to gender studies, which focused on the institutionalized oppression of women. It made it particularly important to her that she could find a means of showing how she remained true to herself. In turn, her husband needed to come to the same realization that the eye makeup was not false and superficial. It was precisely not 'makeup', but the key to who she actually was. Now, the first thing he will remark on and acknowledge is her eye makeup of that day. It is this transformation of her eyes into her truth that becomes, within webcam, the feeling that truth and sincerity are maintained through eye contact, which is how, despite their separation, webcam can become an instrument for coming closer together. All of this is quite deliberate, and corresponds closely to her intellectual working out of what she perceives as the relationship between truth and the self. This is why she will never use 'always-on' webcam. It is only ever face to face and, ideally, eye to eye.

Conclusion

There are several elements to this discovering of the self. The first is visual. What does it mean to *see* ourselves? The second is relational. What does it mean to see ourselves as others see us? Then we also need to consider the implications for our concept of the self. Which idea or whose idea of the self are we talking about? These questions may appear as a vulgarized or literal version of the distinctions that early social theorists such as William James (1890) and G.H. Mead (2009 [1934]) posed to understand the nature of who we are, and which developed into philosophical and psychological debates around topics such as social interactionism. Both these writers distinguished between a concept of *me* and *I*. For Mead, the 'me' certainly derives from experience and interaction, but, as a result of socialization, that largely comes from outside of self-consciousness or reflexivity. By contrast, there is the *I*, as a more active facet of self that is in part a product of our self-awareness or how we imagine we might appear to others. Webcam's impact would be most significant for the further cultivation of this experience of *I*, although this begs the question as to what extent it is our visual aspect, for example, the face itself, that is tantamount to what we think the self is. All of this implies a *self-consciousness* in both the literal and colloquial sense. In turn, this begs a further question of whether a person thinks or feels that this self that they are now more conscious of is more real or true.

As evident from Melchior-Bonnet's (2002) excellent history of the mirror, many myths and moralities have grown up around the issue of reflection, of which Narcissus is only the best known. Plato, who portrays Socrates as positing 'know thyself' as the starting gun for wisdom, saw mere reflection, mainly for its potential for deception as 'specular illusion' (Melchior-Bonnet, 2002: 104–8). If we anticipate that popular discussion of webcam and Facebook will focus on its potential for narcissistic self-regard, or the idea that it replaces a more truthful or actual self, then it is helpful to recall how much the same concerns developed when the production of mirrors became cheap enough to reach the mass population, and, in turn, when photography came to be seen as the democratization of narcissism (Melchior-Bonnet, 2002: 145–55). As noted in Chapter One, technological advances are almost always seen as the loss of authenticity and the true self, mirrors just as much as writing. Advances in the technologies of reflection may also have been debated within the media themselves. Consider the development of both portraiture and reflections on the mirror in Dutch painting from Jan van Eyck to Johannes Vermeer (and Schama, 1987, for how art reflects Dutch society more generally).

So it is possible that this new encounter is profound, but this cannot be presumed and, in any case, in what would this profundity lie? A precedent that clearly understood itself as deeply profound would have been the concept of the mirror stage as developed in the 1970s by Jacques Lacan. This is perhaps the most influential legacy from his corpus of work. The mirror stage was understood as a vital stage in the development of human subjectivity, in that some time after six months of age, a baby becomes able to comprehend themselves as a whole, in contrast to the fragmentary sense of the self they had hitherto experienced. Unfortunately, Lacan deserves a prize for the most pretentious and obscure academic writing of the twentieth century, and it is conveniently hard to interrogate a six-month-old baby to ascertain the consequences of their ability to see themselves from the outside, upon their sense of who or what they are. In any case, as anthropologists, we were never likely to succumb to the temptation to emulate Lacan, whose universalism around a stage in human development rests uneasily next to our emphasis upon cultural relativism.

This was one of the reasons for starting with Colin. As we noted, Colin could be seen as an eccentric individual, or an experimental test of some universal psychological notion of self-consciousness. But actually he only makes sense in relation to particular ways of understanding the self and certain cultural genres of self-expression such as shit-talk. We have to appreciate the cultural genres of normative ways a Trinidadian is expected to present themselves to others, which is why we believe an anthropological perspective is preferable to one derived from philosophy, psychology or psychoanalysis. However, we can still be engaged in conversations between such perspectives and recognize that there are also elements of Colin that express that particular individualism that Cohen (1994) and Rapport (1997) argue can be repressed by anthropological generalization, and also perhaps some elements of universal psychological ideas about the self.

Comparing Isis with Colin, they share the experience that webcam can become the realization and manifestation of a certain kind of truth. For Colin, the emphasis is, as it was with Goffman, on the manipulation of appearance in relation to the other. By contrast, in the case of Isis, there is a greater concern with the integrity of the self, where integrity refers both to cohesion and to truth. While both examples demonstrate the individual's highly creative construction behind the formation of selfhood, we can see that these selves may also strive for the kind of holism that anthropologists traditionally ascribed to society. In contrast to Cohen and Rapport, Bourdieu (1977) showed how an individual becomes typical of their culture by being socialized in a material environment in which there are structural homologies between the order of things, such as house interiors, agricultural cycles and kinship. These common underlying principles of order become the instruments of socialization; the habits and taken-for-granted expectations of normative behaviour that make one person a Kabyle and another person a Tamil. What cases such as Isis suggest is that we need to consider the tension between the holism that anthropologists presume pertains at a social level and that which people may strive for in terms of their own personal integrity, a tension explored recently through various ethnographic examples by Bajic (2009), Botticello (2009), Dalakoglou (2009) and Horst (2009).

It is worth noting that this discussion is far from what used to be seen as the key lessons we should be learning from the development of the internet. At first, reflection on the birth of the internet gave rise to all sorts of discussions about the post-modern and fragmented self that had developed a new capacity for multiple and performative virtual selves. Even at the time, more sustained and sober analyses, such as by Turkle (1984), argued against the hype around this brave new multiple self. These early arguments about anonymity and experimental selves look quite anachronistic today, when people are far more concerned with a loss of anonymity and privacy represented by Facebook. Webcam takes us still further in the opposite direction from these claims about the post-modern self. Along with Facebook, webcam has become an arena of exposure rather than anonymity. This chapter has ended with webcam as a site of personal integrity rather than fragmentation. Occasionally, this stark contrast comes up explicitly in people's personal histories, when they recall nostalgically, or attempt to retain, the freedom they associated with very different kinds of internet usage. For example, 'I didn't want to show myself on webcam because I used to go into chat rooms and like become different people, so like role play in a chat room. I would you know, like talk to people and I remember one person, I had a daughter for some reason so I just made up a random character and you know spoke to people online. So I wasn't really being myself really. And if they asked for a picture I'd find some random picture online and send it, so it's just like a big game with people anywhere in the world that you found in a chat room.' This is a long way from Isis and Margaret.

Finally the evidence in this chapter illustrates the theory of attainment. It is not at all hard to imagine that the things we read about represent concerns and actions regarding the self that humanity in general would always have envisaged doing, but just hadn't previously possessed the technology to realize. We have always been anxious to monitor and transform the self that is seen by others; it's just that previously we were not able to do this. Now thanks to webcam we can. Consistent with the arguments of Chapter One, we have not tried to suggest that webcam makes for a better self or a worse self. Most importantly and foundational to this theory, we have not tried to suggest that webcam makes us more human or less human. Rather, we have tried to acknowledge that, because of this technology, people can do things they previously could not do, although, curiously, this was an unintended side-effect rather than the reason anyone invented this technology. We hadn't envisaged this and, even if we had, the result is always both more and less than our imagination of how it would be.

But is there one more twist to this tale? Could it be that self-consciousness has thereby in some measure actually been increased as well as changed? Following Goody (1977, 1987) and others, we insisted in Chapter One that we must allow for such possibilities. How far webcam is likely to be a profound phase in a more general history of self-consciousness is hard to say. There is also a possible bias in our work. This book is perhaps much too early. It is observing webcam at its moment of birth, still swaddled in our awareness of its conception. If we were instead studying a communication technology that has been present for decades, such as the phone, we would have a very different take on our research. It is possible that this is merely a moment of heightened self-consciousness created by the novelty of the experience. History suggests new forms of communication sink back into the customary with astonishing alacrity. But, it is also possible that, at least to some small extent, we will never see ourselves again in quite the same way. It would be rather premature to conclude either way. We have documented in this chapter the degree to which the people we studied are self-conscious also about being self-conscious. We have given reasons why this might matter, or even matter a great deal. Whether this could be an epochal event in philosophical terms remains to be seen.

3

Intimacy

A key leitmotif in this book is the observation made in Chapter One that studies of digital media are positive to the degree to which they expose the mediated nature of prior communications. They are also negative to the extent that we see the digital as a new form of mediation and lapse into thinking that prior communication was less mediated or unmediated. The suggested precedent for this argument was the work of the sociologist Goffman (1959), who clearly revealed just how much cultural mediation could be found within everyday pre-digital social communication. If, however, there is one field within which there is a particular temptation to resist this contention, it may well be within the arena of intimacy and sex. A reason for tackling intimacy early on is that this is, perhaps, the foundation of the beliefs we wish to expose as false. We will start by considering the various forms of intimacy and love that people experience and how these lead to most taken-for-granted intimacy of constant co-presence for people living together and how these are exposed by the experience of webcam as 'always-on'. We will then be ready to tackle what may seem to be the one irrefutable version of these assumptions, which is that authentic sex depends on the unmediated intimacy of physical co-presence.

The presumption that intimate relationships are the least mediated and therefore the most authentic forms of our social relationships is bolstered by the ideology of romance. It doesn't require much reflection to see how problematic this is. Take, for example, the experience of love. This is quite evidently heavily reliant upon a discourse about love. We are brought up with a whole litany of ideas, expectations, fears and hopes about love, long before we are in a position to actually consider whether we are perhaps falling in love (Beck and Beck-Gernsheim, 1995). The very words 'falling in love' show how far we have set this up as a kind of normative condition, supposedly natural, rather like a benign version of disease that we endeavour to catch.

Anthropologists across the globe (Hirsch and Wardlow, 2006; Donner, 2012) are watching as societies that had traditionally practised arranged marriage or other forms of conjugal life are taking up the ideals of romantic love. But they demonstrate how love operates as quite a clear script mediating the proper form of these new relationships (Collier, 1997; Abu-Lughod, 1998). In Ahearn's (2001) work on Nepali love letters, we can also see that the sign of being modern in the field of love often comes with a commitment to a new media, even, as in this case, when the new media is letter writing – a point that could once have been true of Abélard and Héloïse.

Similarly, when a profession decides it wants to penetrate the façades and defences that mediate our lives in order to expose deep-seated issues and anxieties, psychoanalysts don't assume they are excavating to this bedrock through stripping away mediation. On the contrary, they set up a quite formal frame of the couch, the session, the payment and expectations about transference, in order to find a safe environment from which to enter deeply into the psyche of their patients. Their analyses in turn relate to the fashionable discourses of the day. It would have been hysteria in the nineteenth century, but not today. In short, psychoanalysis is a form of, rather than a removal of, mediation. This was a major component of our theory of attainment, that we should stop thinking we are studying whether communication is more or less mediated, and instead examine the changes in mediation as an intrinsic component of communication.

So, when it comes to webcam there will, of course, be a popular discourse that sees this as a technical mediation that makes it less intimate also because it is somehow less open, less true, or just less of a relationship. Yet even within the practice of anthropology, we find examples where webcam emerges as the more immediate and rich environment for intimacy in contrast to physical co-presence. A convenient example is currently emerging from the work of Tiziana Traldi, a PhD student of Miller.[1] Having a child of her own, it was difficult for her to spend as much time as she would have liked being ethnographically present in the houses of her informants in Italy. Her informants were also mothers, whose relation to their children was the topic of her study. She therefore took up webcamming, more for logistical reasons of convenience than anything else. This was despite the scepticism of some anthropologists who told her this could not be counted as authentic fieldwork, because she was not actually with her informants. As it happens, she had already spent quite some time in conventional co-present fieldwork with those mothers in their homes. She was therefore able to make a direct comparison. She found that these mothers often revealed much more about themselves, and were much more personal, when she talked with them, often for hours, through webcam, compared to when she had been with them in their homes. Miller has speculated (whereas Traldi is more cautious) that perhaps this is linked to the Italian tradition of confession, which makes the mediated exchange of webcam a more natural environment within which to reveal things about themselves that otherwise might have remained hidden.

A similar point would also follow from Miller and Slater's discussion of religion in Trinidad in their book *The Internet: An Ethnographic Approach* (2000: 173–95). In fieldwork with Catholic Charismatics, they saw the advent of email as providing a depth of spiritual encounter that had no precedent. Letters between people in different Caribbean islands were hopeless, since by the time you had a reply, you were out of synch with the question. Yet, face-to-face encounters contain an element of superficiality. For, when someone is speaking to you face to face, this demands a relatively instant, and therefore potentially less considered, response. But deep spiritual matters require contemplation, often several hours of introspection. Email gave space for this pause, while remaining within the temporality of true engagement and so led to more profound discussions than the precedents of either letters or face-to-face conversation.

[1]Tiziana Traldi is currently a PhD student of Miller and we are grateful for permission to cite her unpublished work.

The crucial point is that it will not help us to understand webcam if we start by regarding it as some poor, or even good, approximation to forms of intimacy whose foundation and authenticity lie in co-presence. Our opening example of Samantha and Oreal will help us transcend such an assumption, because it is clear that they don't view webcam contact as some kind of secondary presence. They simply integrate it, as mere medium, into what really matters for them, which is intimacy itself.

Samantha and Oreal

Most studies of migration assume that people come to affluent countries in search of high living standards. Many do, but academics may have underestimated the degree to which people migrate in order to escape from some troubling personal issue back home, such as having just dumped a boyfriend who still lives in the same village. Oreal lives in the US, but the reason she left Trinidad at the age of 17 was because she couldn't bear the consequences of having had a child from a married man who didn't leave his wife. The US is not a promised land, but a land of exile, and every day she craves contact with her own people. Perhaps, as a result, she has made hardly any friends within the US, where she remains lonely and unfulfilled.

Fortunately, if you are in the position of Oreal and are desperate for a daily slice of Trinidad life, then her best friend Samantha is the perfect correspondent. It is partly that Samantha seems to embody all that vibrancy that Oreal sees as quintessentially Trinidadian and so lacking in the US. With her coiffured hair, great nails, bright clothes and still brighter manner, Samantha is full of life. But equally important, Samantha has a salon. This equates with salon as in hairdressing, massage, waxes, facials and general cosmetic treatments – a one-stop shop for all matters of female beautification. But this is also a salon in the traditional Parisian mode, a place where people come to gossip and socialize.

It's hard to say which of these two ducks took more readily to the water of webcam; whether it was Oreal's need to see, or Samantha's need to be seen. After all, Samantha's work is so visual. One of the major subcultures of the YouTube generation is that of the cosmetic gurus, who advise fellow teenagers on what to apply and how (Spyer, 2011). Samantha may not be aware of them, but on her own account she fully appreciates that online is a great place to show off her skills in nail art or the use of certain polishes. And just as in the salon, none of this happens without a running conversation, which flits between commentary upon what she is doing and everything else under the sun. All sorts of social butterflies and unlikely moths flutter around the light of Samantha's webcam, from friends in New York to a male soldier in London. She keeps this online presentation discrete; she displays makeup and manicures, but certainly no massages. When there is no one in the salon and nothing to exhibit, she relapses into general chit-chat online, which equally reflects the physical salon, as customers stay for hours beyond their given appointment to talk about problems in their family or how a celebrity looked on television the night before.

The webcam in question is within a laptop and quite mobile. When Samantha wants to stretch her legs and take a walk around the mall, within which her salon is situated, she may on occasion take the laptop also to show someone what shops have closed and which have opened. Mostly, her friends are intermittent, getting on with their work and, like Samantha, fitting these webcam sessions opportunistically into the interstices of life. There is one exception to this and that is Oreal. In her case, it's not so much the webcam, but the person, who could be described as always-on. Oreal has children but nothing seems to get in the way of her craving to be back in Trinidad and back with Samantha. As Samantha notes of exiles such as Oreal, 'they are Trini to the bone. So they just wanna see what goes on, even though they are up there . . . Oreal says life over there is so easy for her with the kids, but she's quite lonely. She's locked up in a house, and she's always on. If I go on now, she's on, she's always on, always looking out to see when I'm coming on, yes.'

Of course, they used to talk before the advent of webcam, but then given how 'loooong' they talked, they were forever checking that the phone card was not about to run out. In addition, there is so much more they can do with webcam. With webcam, 'she shows me around her place where she's renting, and it's much fun, you get to talk more, yeah, because I Skype her even from home. So I walk around with my little cam and she gets to see my house, yeah, so it's fun, it's much fun.'

Actually, it takes a whole lot of mobile webcam just to show Samantha herself:

> I show every single detail, step by step. So it's like I pick up the camera and I move around, so it's not like, you're not seeing my face alone, you're seeing every part of me, because I show her my toes and I do my toes, everything, down to my tattoo . . . She gets to hear the music, the parang, calypso. So I shared everything. When I bought my vehicle I showed her . . . And there's this guy that she likes, who fixed my AC at home, and she say she still loves him. So every time he comes over to do the repairs I have him chatting with her, I have him chatting with her, so they get to catch up too, yes. So every time he comes over, and she always says 'make sure when he coming, call me you know, call me', because she's always on, she's always on.

What the webcam also provides is not so much the face to face as the heart to heart. Left to themselves, Oreal tends rather quickly to tears. Samantha notes:

> I keep telling her, I say 'gyurl [girl] yuh need to come back home, come back home and you'll enjoy it' and then she'll get over and she'll say she'll come and you know, cheer her up. It's sad because knowing that she's far away, we cannot do all the stuff that we used to do growing up, and her life is totally different where she have to take care of her children . . . So I tell her I say 'hear it, yuh done have a chile, yuh made a mistake, yuh gonna hang on, yuh have to do the best for your daughter, since it's a girl you have, she's gonna look up at you, and you're going to show her you're better than that' and this is where I comfort her, you know I cheer her up. I say 'hey, when yuh come Trinidad, we're gonna do our toes, we're gonna do our nails, we're gonna have some fun'. Yes, because if I break down and cry with her, I mean to say we'll stay there for hours crying, for what sense, right. Because I'm older than her and I have to show her, well ok I have been through a failed marriage, I have 2 other children with a failed marriage . . . there's life after, there's better life after, you have to want it. So it's like I show her my experience and encourage her to do better. Now she's going back to school. She told me she took up extra classes, plus she's learning to do nails, so that when she comes to Trinidad she could do my nails and she could make extra money and cut costs because it's very expensive over there to have her nails done. So I

> kinda encourage her to do a lot of stuff . . . Because it's like you have to hug the screen and it's like you know, I'll send kisses for her and 'stop crying I'm here' and a couple times I scream and say 'STOP CRYING! It's not the end of the world, get up you're a woman, woman fall if they allow themselves. Get up! Move on!'

Samantha has to believe that webcam works as an effective conduit to the hearts and minds of others. The salon was never just about physical things:

> When somebody comes for the first time and they start talking to me, I will sit down and I will look at you, and by looking at you, you could say well ok she have some problems, we need to talk to her, and then from there, because the majority of the time people come in, especially at salons, women talk their personal business, well in Trinidad, this is what they say, gossip, they talk their personal business with their therapist and they ask advice, majority of the time, right, and this is where they come close to their personal therapist. So even though it's via webcam, you can tell still if there's a problem with the person, because with her I can tell.

Webcam is no impediment, because it is so revealing. There is the expression on the face, the tone in the voice and especially the state of the makeup. There is the sense of desperation and the need to talk. All of this conveys what Samantha calls an energy state that allows her to weigh up the problems and find something that can help restore the balance. But then this was equally true in the salon. The massages and the nails and the hair are merely the tip of a less tangible force, a mass of conversation, sympathetic ears, aesthetic appraisal, female solidarity that pours into, through and out of webcams to bring a closeness that most people will never experience, however much they can physically touch each other. For Samantha and Oreal, intimacy is not a question of what a webcam can and cannot do. Intimacy is question of what a Trini can and cannot do.

Always-on

From early on in our research, it was evident that there were two radically different ways in which people could use webcam.

The previous chapter on self-consciousness emphasized how, typically, webcam is even more in one's face than co-presence, a de-contextualized mutual staring between correspondents. As the technology has become more reliable, it is also possible to simply leave webcams on in the background, while going about one's general household activities such as cleaning, cooking or studying, without directly paying attention to the other person, remaining aware of where they are and what they are doing. It is possible to graduate to this 'always-on' webcam for hours, without having any direct conversation at all.

As such, webcam has highlighted two very different versions of strong intimacy. The intimacy of intense communication and the intimacy of taking for granted the co-presence of the other. This second form is obviously analogous to the experience of two people merely living together in the same place. As it happened, two of the earliest cases studied by Miller and Madianou during their research on migration (Madianou and Miller, 2012a) had pointed to an important possible consequence of this distinction. The first case consisted of a separated couple who understood webcam as visual telephony and only ever used it for face-to-face conversation. It was clear that they found this necessity of constantly having to respond to each other, faces pressed almost against each other through the screen, and the resulting intensity of this kind of intimacy, something of a burden over time. The second case was an early instance of always-on webcam. The webcam remained on largely as background in order to reproduce the experience of domestic co-presence, without any expectation of constant acknowledgement and response. Miller predicted at that time, correctly, that the first couple would break up, while the second would survive.

Always-on is still relatively new. Only around a fifth of the people we worked with seem to have any experience of it, while few use it with any constancy. Our own experience is that Skype remains relatively unreliable and tends to fail after a while. This initial generalization based on these two cases was obviously too simplistic, but always-on is a profoundly different way of using, and even thinking about, webcam and its potential. It is worth dwelling upon it because it seems probable that as the technology improves further, it will become far more important. Indeed, it is entirely possible that one day the normal mode of webcam use will be much closer to always-on, rather than our current model of video telephony.

The idea of webcam as video telephony is a good example of what Bolter and Grusin (2000) called remediation. In short, we tend to think of the new media, at least initially, as the latest iteration of some prior media. Accordingly, webcam is generally first understood as a telephone, with an additional visual component. Later on, when always-on webcam becomes common, the webcam is likely to find its own niche as a more autonomous and original form of sociality, though still connected with precedence, but in the future that may be the prior experience of residential co-presence. At the moment, we may be in a more experimental period. An example we encountered in fieldwork was the idea of always-on as a kind of virtual date. A couple would decide, quite self-consciously, to try to have a 'date' via webcam. This was rare and mainly consisted of couples deciding to simultaneously watch a movie or television series. For example, 'If there is a part in the movie that catches her attention, she will pause it and send me a message "this part looking real good" like that. I personally, don't really talk. I wait for the end of the movie then talk.' Our general impression was that dating via webcam remained somewhat awkward and not overly successful.

By contrast, virtual eating together and indeed virtual falling asleep together seemed to drift more obviously into always-on as virtual co-habitation. In several instances, what was striking was that living together through webcam could develop for a couple who, while they had had sex before their separation, hadn't actually lived together. Webcam proved surprisingly adept at effectively introducing them to this possibility. This was the case for a Brazilian couple who had only spent a month together before she came to London.

> I'm like 'I'm going to show you something really disgusting' and I show him and I say 'look at these hairs, how dare they?' Then he says 'I am going to puke! . . .' We got to know so much more about each other. Where I knew I am a messy person normally, I tried to be less messy. And he noticed and said 'Oh wow! You're being much less messy than normal! . . .' It's weird when it's on your webcam because you're peeing and you're like 'Don't listen! Don't listen!' on the webcam, and you're just like – this is ridiculous. He

> just laughs. He just says 'I won't!', then I say 'OK I'm done! Let's clean this bathroom!' *[So there is some embarrassment]* Of course! Just like there would be normally. But then at a point, that was the first time, then I thought either I don't take it in and just tell him I'm going to the toilet but *[Wait just to check, when you're on webcam with him do you always take the laptop into the bathroom with you or just sometimes?]* Sometimes, other times it feels weird, and then I'll just say 'Wait a sec, I'm going to the toilet, give me two seconds', but then sometimes I'll come back and he won't be there, which is really weird.

Such reportage suggests that always-on webcam can effectively reproduce the grounded experience of intimacy as the initial period of learning to live together. In one transnational case of a relationship that lasted around six months, always-on was their only experience of 'living together,' since they broke up before this could be reproduced offline. Again, we might speculate that this is a harbinger of future genres of relationship development.

For younger people, the most common form of always-on seemed to be having webcam in the background. This tended to be part of polymedia (see Chapter Six), in that they would simultaneously have Facebook and other applications open. The various media just formed part of the constant play of attention between different people and tasks. A very common example was the way students do their homework, once it had migrated largely to online activity, then became a natural part of such multi-tasking, being conducted alongside all sorts of other activities and people. With older informants, the most common activity mentioned as occupying always-on time was cooking. At present, this seemed to be regarded as normal if the correspondent is living abroad, but perhaps a bit peculiar if the person is living in the same country.

Several people specifically reject always-on as an option: 'It's always face to face. Most of the time I prefer to talk to him face to face, cos I miss him, so I want to give him my attention.' Or 'The only time we really Skype, it's to talk to one another, it's not to just have me on Skype on a call and I'm seeing them doing the dishes or something. It's not like that. Whenever we are on Skype, we are talking to each other and when we finish, that's it.' Some mix and match: 'Between 2 and a half to 3 hours, 50 per cent face to face, the other time, looking at other programs, doing other things, watching movies.'

Chelsea and Avi are a good example of a couple who survived the separation of one partner, spending years abroad at university. As in our original prediction, webcam seemed most effective when it became a taken-for-granted aspect of easy co-presence. When living together, they would always try to have their meals together, which led them to replicate this custom through webcam. The intimacy of co-presence is perhaps greatest when there is no pressure to make it explicit:

> When someone is with you and you're not always looking at them, but you know they are there – it was like that . . . On Skype just the idea of him always being around – like I'm changing my clothes and then I'm like 'Oh, hi, you're on Skype!' And I didn't even realize. So it still happened . . . because it was right next to my bed. So several times when it was on, I was like, this is my pillow, this is yours, and he would do the same thing. Sometimes I would ask him which side of the bed are you sleeping on? And it was a real comfort to me . . . So I would Skype him and say 'I'm going to sleep now, I need you to come on Skype'. I would say stuff like that. I would be sleeping and if I turned to my right which I usually would, I would see him sleeping right next to me.

This was something they had rarely had the opportunity to do before she left Trinidad. Similarly, a wife tried to express her need for her husband's webcam presence as follows: 'I could be in the safest places and I would still be afraid. Not afraid, but just lonely, I prefer the company. I prefer the feeling of somebody there, and that's what Skype does. The part that it's free means that he could just be there without talking and I could just know I could be able to go on about this, or how to fix this, or how to turn this on, and he is right there.'

Always-on as co-habitation is not confined to couples, as for many Trinidadians, whose first experience of living abroad alone is as students, what they miss most is the comfort and support of family life. This same female student also uses webcam to try to bring back the intimacy of relaxed co-presence with her family. 'That happened often and then sometimes I'd just be listening to music, they'd be listening to music, and they're always watching shows on the internet, and we'd be chatting between and talking about the same things we'd been watching.' Having never lived outside of a family environment often meant that being abroad represented loneliness and stress. 'Because I came from Trinidad in a house where you can't even get enough space to breathe. And all of a sudden it warps into this quiet space, and that was rough for me.' What she needed was a sense of her sister's presence. 'I may be lying down and reading a book and trying to study and she would just be online. It just felt good to me at that time to have a support system present in some kind of way. And that is what it meant to me to have somebody online . . . to feel like I wasn't alone in my apartment. And that I could access somebody if need be.' Similarly, a Trini woman says, 'I've never actually felt like it was being intrusive, because if it was up to my father he would be on FaceTime with us all day long.' In fact, it is only her mother who stops her father from trying to webcam her incessantly. iPads have proved popular with an older demographic. So we can imagine the spread of FaceTime having this sort of consequence far more frequently in the future.

Different media have different analogies to this potential of always-on media. McCarthy (2001) studies television not as something we necessarily watch but as the ambient background to social life. Indeed, in many countries TV simply remains on all day. In Trinidad, music is pretty much a constant background presence and Trinidadians may seem uncomfortable trying to socialize when there is no music on without realizing why they are feeling so awkward. Closer to the webcam example is the idea of mobile phones as 'perpetual contact' (Katz and Aakhus, 2002) that allows people to feel that they are always at least within reach of the other, something that Pertierra (pers. comm.) suggests is true even for texting in the Philippines. These are precedents but with webcam the cycle seems to turn further back to the experience of actually living together.

To conclude, all our evidence suggests that always-on is likely to grow into one of the most significant uses of webcam in the future. It seems entirely possible that even the gradual life-cycle of a couple, from meeting to dating, to 'sort-of' cohabitation and then to separation, may start to be viable without ever actually meeting, partly because webcam seems to reflect something that many people would in any case have asserted about intimacy itself. In marked contrast to the last chapter, some of the most complete forms of intimacy are about not just the loss of self-consciousness, but the general easing away from any imperative to communicate. Ironically, it is when a communication device morphs into a reason for not having to communicate that webcam will become most successful. It will instead constitute the supportive condition of simply knowing that someone else is there – if and when.

This is also one of the clearest examples of how a new digital technology helps us to reflect upon the prior form of sociality and realize how we had failed to pierce the presumptions that lay beneath its normative presence. This is because 'always-on' webcam often attempts to re-construct the intimacy of 'natural' co-presence; two people in the same house and sharing the same rooms. It is only with the advent of webcam that we come to appreciate the quite bizarre nature of living together under the same roof. We can be in exactly the same space but carefully not acknowledging each other, or determining the exact degree of balance between acknowledgment and aversion. We can also have created intimacy as a mode which is constituted by not requiring overt communication. Always-on webcam suddenly makes us realize that there could have been a whole other study analogous to the corpus of work by Goffman (1959). Goffman exposed the underlying and unspoken frames of encounter in the public domain, while always-on webcam suggests another research project to expose the underlying and unspoken frames of living together in the private sphere.

Other forms of intimacy

We have argued that, paradoxically, always-on can be most effective as intimacy, precisely because intimacy becomes taken for granted, without requiring overt expression. Yet, there are many other possibilities for intimacy. Perhaps the opposite of always-on is when people try to ignore its technological limitations, for the most literal expressions of affection: for example, when someone tells us that their family was particularly tactile, so that when on webcam there would be endless hugging of the camera, putting arms around the screen, kissing the surface or touching it with their fingertips. Another noted that adults felt a bit stupid doing this, but their daughters loved kissing and hugging the technology and expected lots of waving and air kissing in return. More reticent correspondents may hope, as they put it, to caress with words and gestures, through facial expressions and tone of voice. There is also the option of stressing the undivided attention of the face-to-face videophone in preference to always-on.

Another way of indicating intimacy can be through the position of the webcam and the laptop. It was quite common for people to webcam from their bed with the laptop on their stomach. For English males, this indicates sloth rather than intimacy, but for a Trinidadian female, it can be part of an attempt to replicate one of the most intimate aspects of a relationship which for them was not sex, but simply going to sleep beside each other. There still remain practical problems, for example, having enough light, the sliding-off laptop, and its weight. Physical co-presence can also prevent intimacy, as when places are shared and someone else walks past in the background, just as the conversation was going somewhere. To balance these positives, we should note that physicality was discussed a good deal more often as an example of the limitations of webcam. Hugging a screen was not like hugging a person; it reminded you that you couldn't actually touch and perhaps missed that tactile element to the relationship even more. Just as you were becoming reconciled to separation, webcam reminds you of what you can no longer do or be, although there were some who had been unwilling to become physically close prior to webcam, which seemed to them a safer, more comfortable, place to develop intimacy.

Ann says of her cousin:

> Well, she is not a person to really use a lot of words, she's more conservative. But by her expressions and everything, we could just know what she means or how touchy the subject is or things like that . . . She's not the type of person where she would like you to comfort her a lot or anything, probably just like say one thing. Sometimes not say anything, just be there and eventually change the topic, or talk about something else. We real mushy, so we'll just watch each other and probably make sad noises and it would turn into a joke . . . She would be on her bed, so the laptop is on top of her, yeah it is kind of intimate. Yeah in Trinidad we usually sleep on the same bed, when we have sleepovers, we're really close. Yeah and I would do the same thing [have the laptop with her in bed]. I use a directory, it's kinda heavy but it's stable.

Ann herself had recently met a man whom, since he was a year ahead of her in his studies, it seemed natural to make into a sort of mentor. After a while, these conversations became more personal, and they were exchanging other confidences, and it was clear that a mutual crush was developing. Through Skype, Ann feels a sense of being in his home, while this might be too early in their relationship to actually go there with him. She shares a room, which leads her to keep her voice low and use headphones, but this actually makes the exchange feel more, rather than less, intimate. It creates a softness in her voice that feels just right. At school, they feel awkward, spending long times together in the public eye. By contrast, on webcam, they can talk about work for hours and feel more in control. Webcam allows things to progress in a manner that feels natural and appropriate, while it is the physically co-present where things seem artificial and forced.

For established couples, relationships have already become embedded not just in physical things, but in familiar routines and expressions that had become integral to living together. In the evening, they might just have a little chat, an 'I love you', or a debriefing of the stressful and irritating things that had happened at work that day. 'Just talk about each other's days, "What have you been up to today sweetie?" you know "I've been up to this, that and this", "anything out of the ordinary happen?" just talking, you know, all the mushy stuff and yeah "Goodnight".' For others, the key moment is the wakeup call, the need to have seen them before going to work. 'It doesn't have to be a formal discussion, OK, let's sit down and have a conversation', but a greeting in the morning, a simple by-the-way comment, that is important. Sometimes it's banter and the way he makes fun of her being a bit of a drama queen by waving his palms downwards to calm her down. Not surprisingly, the emphasis on having just a few key moments, or phrases, works best for long established couples. A man married for 34 years feels his wife is his best friend, with whom he shares everything, but he has to travel abroad for work. 'When I talk to my wife on my webcam I am not feeling sad. I am happy, I am glad to talk to her. It puts my mind at ease and in my hotel room I can lie down and sleep comfortably . . . We just communicate to talk to one another, make sure everything is alright, just to have a friendly conversation.'

Webcam simply doesn't work for everyone, and some don't find it a comfortable medium for intimacy. As one woman noted about a very close friend, 'on camera she becomes awkward and introverted. She is quieter and the conversation becomes more stilted and formal, and it always amazes me, cause if I Skype her this week and we have that kind of toned down conversation, and the next month she come and visit. And I think hmm, I wonder how this going to be, is it going to be weird. And it is perfectly normal and she is back to talkin' loud and bein' herself.' In this case, it is the technology that is experienced as intimidating and oppressive. For others, webcam is no limitation to becoming emotional and expressive, as one boyfriend found when his girlfriend was trying to get things off her chest, and was getting very heated, crying and making what he saw as wild gestures, until he felt he literally had to back off away from the screen. By the same token, a woman who knows this can be off-putting states, 'I'm a very emotional person, all the time. So like I would tend to try and filter so many things I would have to say, or how I say it, because I don't want to come across as too strong or too emotionally overbearing.'

Reviewing this wide range of possible responses to webcam, the critical factor is usually whether the two partners are in synch. It may be fine if they both like to be overtly emotional, and equally fine if they both dislike such behaviour. What matters most is whether they respect each other's response:

> Yeah, his approach is more, he always tells me that it's more difficult for him, cos he's there alone. And I'm here with the kids, with my family and his family, while he is there on his own. It's more difficult for him to get so worked up about seeing you and interacting with you and whatever. His approach is more casual because he knows what he has to deal with on a daily basis. Whereas my approach is, we have to be close. We are more in sync now. It has been two years, so we are much better than when we started.

Finally, there is the issue of whether the response to the technology dominates or is subservient to the sense of the relationship that is carried by the technology. This varies, but a useful insight into this contradiction came through Delicia, who was one of the not small number of technophobes in our study, in the sense of someone who actively dislikes technology. She mainly uses webcam after her own child has gone to bed, in order not to be a bad influence on her. She worries about privacy, she worries about anonymity and she worries about strangers online. Most such technophobes also tend to believe there are health issues, radiation or cancer, or similar negative consequences (Brosnan, 1998). Despite all this, Delicia is an inveterate user of all media technologies and regularly contacts her 14–16-year-old students through webcam, but also Facebook, email and MSN. To understand this paradox, we have to reflect on why people like Delicia dislike such technologies. Typically, they fear that technology detracts from personhood and the more intimate and personal aspects of relationships. Delicia would expect that the people who dislike technology are those who are most warm to other people.

For example, Delicia has a real feel for students. She has noticed that in the class they are hesitant when discussing Shakespeare, and tend to be relatively formal, but online they are more at ease and forthcoming. One reason for this, she explains, is that students are more comfortable using colloquial speech patterns and spelling online, since this is how they would almost always write online; so a student might say in class, 'Yes Miss, I understand,' but that evening, online, they would say, 'Miss, dis is rel mess!' She sees that they are more open and honest online. Furthermore, in class, they are intimidated by the presence of their peers, while online they feel no pressure if the only person they are speaking to is Delicia. She uses communication to come close, and has no fear regarding the intrusive consequences of being constantly available to her students. In short, this fear and dislike of technology derives from a fearless fondness for people, and, of the two, it is the latter that is so much more important. Paradoxically, technophobes sometimes make much more use of communication technologies than technophiles. Madianou and Miller (2012a), in their study of Filipina mothers in the UK with children left behind in the Philippines, found that necessity and desire can often make technophobes the vanguard when it comes to developing the potential of new media.

The intimacy that people try to reproduce or create through webcam has, then, several components. The most literal and physical modes range from gestures to the positioning of the camera. Intimacy may equally be manifest through routines or even just showing how the other is taken for granted as a presence. Yet, we will only appreciate intimacy if we focus as much on aspects of the relationship, such as emotionality and closeness, as on properties of the media such as visibility. It is the combination of all of these that constitutes viability in separated relationships, as we can see in the case of Monique.

Monique

Monique, who we will meet again in the next chapter, gives us that more holistic, ethnographic sense of the way all such the physical and relational elements come together in the maintenance of a long-distance relationship. As in many of these previous cases, the word that stands for such transcendent and holistic experience is simply – love.

Though, in practice, it has taken a while for Monique to find a balance between webcam as face to face, and webcam as always on.

> I think we just end up like, OK he'll tell me about his day and I'll say about my day, and we would stare at each other for a while, like literally just stare, and I'd be like 'OK I gonna try to write my introduction now' or before it would be like 'I gonna try to read this for class tomorrow' and he'd be like 'OK' or he'd be like 'yeah I'm gonna mark some papers' or 'I'm gonna go shave' or something, and he'll just leave it in the background.

Then sometimes they may be on the phone forgetting that the webcam is there in the background and that they could just as well have been speaking through that.

> I dunno but when we leave it in the background, I literally get up and move away and do something else. Yeah well when we started, we used to kinda fall asleep and leave Skype on, that kinda thing, because he just likes the idea of it being on, and I guess I like the idea of it being on, and knowing that he's sleeping and I'm sleeping. I'll go to sleep first, it's actually him, he's kinda creepy like that, he likes watching me sleep, so it was more for him, and I guess as I was here for the first time kinda alone. I guess he felt like he was watching over me, so it was that kinda taking care of me aspect,

> because I still sleep with night lights, so it's not like it's utter darkness. But when I get up he will obviously be sleeping and I'll just see this darkness on the screen. Yeah, and sometimes I'll shout, I used to shout and be like 'get up!' That would be like 4 o'clock in the morning Trinidad time and his hair would all be messy and everything, and his eyes, and he would be like 'yeah, I'm up, I'm up'. I don't know, why I did it . . . but it was just pure wickedness to me . . . and then he has these very fluffy cheeks, and he fluffs up more on mornings, and then his hair is all just all over and down in his face, because he has his hair grown kinda long.

Not surprisingly, the field of food and cooking also brings out the banter and affection between them. The webcam is often on when they are cooking.

> Sometimes I show him what I made. Well he's evil as well, because I like Bar-B-Que from the real Bar-B-Que hut in San Fernando and he'll be like 'oh, I'm gonna get some Bar-B-Que today' and I'll be like 'OK, what are you gonna have' and he'll be like 'maybe chicken' and I'm not fazed by chicken and then he'll say 'maybe some lamb' and I'll be like 'Oh OK' and he's like 'and some pasta salad' and he knows that's my combination, so he'll get it and he'll show me it. So the next day I'll make something that he likes. So I'll make lasagne and I'll show him and I'll be like 'Ooh all this lasagne for me, little old me' and I'll eat it in front of him . . . Sometimes what will happen is he'll eat breakfast and I'll eat lunch . . . I'll be like 'Oh I made burgers' but I made my patties myself and I could guarantee you it's 98 per cent meat, no fillers. And I'll show him, and recently I made one and I put cheese in the middle, he always wanted me to put cheese for it to get melty, and I showed him, and I cut it, and I'm like 'see how it's melty.' So I made it and I put pine and everything and I made a fry egg as well and I showed him, and I stacked it up, and I showed him how it was melty and he was like 'well I have to go' (she laughs loudly) but I promised I would make it for him when I get back.

Ultimately, though, she is just as clear on Skype's limitations, for example, when he had problems. 'So it was hard for him, and you can't hug somebody via Skype, you could say "OK fine, it'll be fine" no pat on the back or anything. So it's one thing to see somebody but it's another thing to comfort somebody and to be with somebody. Sometimes we say "yeah thank goodness for

Skype" and then sometimes we say "Oh Skype doesn't really cut it at this point".'

Sex

Sex has always been in the vanguard of online technological developments; webcam is still associated with the phenomenon of camgirls (Senft, 2008), pornography and other ways in which webcam aids masturbation singly or mutually. Our research was more focused upon relationships and wider issues of intimacy, especially the viability of long-distance and longer term relationships. We feel that now we have established this emphasis, it is safe to confront sex more directly without it dominating our discussion. It is an essential element not just for many of our informants but also as a core example of the presumption of physical co-presence. The absence of sex is potentially a hugely damaging and debilitating consequence of that separation, which has become an increasingly common consequence of global migration, subsequent upon developments in the political economy. If webcam becomes important in repairing this wound, then that is something we should perhaps both welcome and try to understand. This provides us with a more empathetic vision than a literature that sometimes becomes the voyeuristic study of webcam voyeurism, though that too is something we will need to confront.

Those who would see webcam as the sign of ever increasing mediation within modern sex assume that it facilitates an increasing use of fantasy. But this is highly unlikely, given the results of Kahr's (2007) extensive study of the reliance of everyday co-present sexual relations on fantasy. Kahr's work comprehensively demonstrates that it is actually long established co-present couples who may have become most reliant upon fantasy. Years away from the initial erotic encounter, couples sustain sex with their now taken-for-granted partner, largely through simultaneously fantasizing about other persons as new and fresh sexual objects, in their heads. Kahr also reveals that these can include sexual scenarios, such as incest or violence, that would be quite unacceptable anywhere other than in fantasy. So far from being free from mediation, such couples probably wouldn't now be able to have successful co-present sex without this mediation of fantasy.

In addition, we have evidence from Slater's (1998) early work on online pornography. He showed how trading 'sexpics' – sexually explicit images – was often the work of housewives looking for erotic additions to bring to the routines of well-established couples, and the surrounding conversations were more about establishing than refusing moral boundaries. Ben-Ze'ev's (2004) exploration of online sex within established relationships makes similar points to those within this chapter, though he adds several dimensions such as whether people regard non-partner online sex as adultery, and the extent to which it is used to complement offline sex with alternative sexual activity. In contrast to both his and our study, Kaufmann (2012) tends to regard online encounters as new forms of mediation, which detract from the authenticity of prior forms of intimacy and sexual relations. In our case, we have tried to contextualize sex by first dealing with the non-erotic forms of intimacy. We now try to make a series of points with respect to sex itself through the juxtaposition and sequences of the following four characters, Shantel, Stephanie, Donovan and Tonia.

Shantel

You only need look at Shantel's Facebook page to realize that sooner or later the subject of sex is likely to emerge. Whenever she meets someone new, one of the first pictures that she somehow gets around to showing them from Facebook is a photo shoot to advertise a club night. In fishnet stockings, with cane and hat, the scene is something between cabaret and burlesque. It's not overly raunchy, but she clearly feels this was the sexiest picture ever taken of her, and is how she really wants to see herself and for others to see her. What she is most proud of is the way she is developing skills around cosmetics and the other arts of looking good. It comes from her upbringing. Her mother was devoted to Carnival and there are many Trinidadians for whom the rest of the year is really just a pause, as they wait for the time when they can 'play themselves' because they primarily identify with the Carnival butterfly, not the drab caterpillar they must play the rest of the year. In her time, Shantel has tried a bit of modelling and some photography as well as developing her skills in makeup, all in addition to her regular job. Before Carnival, she will use webcam to show this year's costume to her mother and aunt abroad, knowing they will respond with some comment about how this skimpy little thing could hardly be called a costume. Webcam also helps her to show friends from abroad the range of costumes to choose from.

Webcam has been integral to her life for six years, ever since her mother migrated to New York, but she, at the age of 22, decided not to join her. She has no regrets about the decision, noting that even her relationship with her mother has improved. Her mother never was that sensitive a parent, and this combination of autonomy and contact has produced about the best parental role that she was ever likely to assume. If anything, she is closer to her aunt, also in the US. Their webcamming can sometimes amount to a three-hour session. There is also a scattering of around ten friends and relatives living in the US and England that she keeps in touch with through webcam. She also uses webcam regularly in her work, where the purchasing department interacts with foreign traders. This loops back to Carnival, as some of her work friends formed a carnival section within a band. They employ Skype, firstly because it's free, secondly so they can discuss as a group rather than separate dyads, and finally because this visual media is essential when the conversation is mainly about their costumes. Indeed, it's already hard to imagine how they ever did without it.

While this is not something she ever envisaged, Shantel was therefore more likely to at least entertain the prospect of a webcam relationship than most. Not surprisingly, this started as a little Carnival something, with a Jamaican guy who was just over for the two weeks. Nothing serious, but they exchanged numbers. In fact, things only really started to develop as they came to know each other better through Skype, and found themselves talking every day and every night. It took a couple of months to reach this point, which they sustained for around six months. She says she was a little bit shy about the turn to the physical at first, but we are guessing not much. Skype worked well as sex and there was no problem attaining orgasm. The main restraint is very understandable once you know about the huge attachment she feels for Anya Ayoung-Chee, a Trinidadian ex-Miss Universe contestant, whose private sex tape had been leaked to the internet.

Anya Ayoung-Chee had recently become, for a third time, the biggest thing in Trinidad, when she won the US TV competition *Project Runway* with her clothing designs. Shantel, whose ethnic makeup clearly includes Chinese, is happy for people to see her as an Anya clone; she even does her hair Anya style. Even so, she has no desire to follow her idol in suffering the scandal of a public sex tape. It was essential to first establish a strong sense of trust, because only then could she be at ease with her Jamaican partner. It wasn't that she ever taped any of these sessions, just a fear that he might, without telling her.

Given the extent of her previous experience, it's not likely that Shantel had much to learn about sex from cybersex, though she does say it taught her some new things about her body. The real revelation came more from the non-physical aspects. As Shantel admits, up until then, so much of life consisted of going out, meeting a guy, drinking, having fun and having sex, none of which necessarily involved a whole lot of talking, but when you get to know someone online, then most of what is happening is not physical, it's verbal. Even the sex itself depends largely on one's ability to describe and discuss what each wants from the other and what turns them on.

As she puts it:

> So most of our time spent together was talking to each other and getting to know each other, and know each other's different moods; what we're doing all day, who we met and you know just like things we do – and it was actually really nice. I guess that's why it lasted for that long, because I got to just come home and talk to somebody who would actually listen to me. And the difference is if I was with somebody right here, right now, we would be more physical, instead of getting to talk to each other, knowing our different habits. You know what I mean, or just talking, we would be more physical. And with him I get to learn a lot just by all the conversations I had. You know we just find more interesting things to talk about and laugh and you know just enjoy a conversation, learn to converse with somebody without being physical 100 per cent.

Shantel paid one visit to Jamaica, but it was expensive, she knew no one else there, and neither would have moved country for the other. After that six months, she met someone locally and ended this online relationship. There was a real irony to this. Far from constituting a reduction to sex (Kaufmann, 2012), cybersex was Shantel's first introduction to the potential of wider relationships, based on getting to know someone through talking. Yet at the same time, as month after month went by, she missed the physicality of co-present sex, which was probably one of the factors leading her to find an alternative partner. She says, 'The downside (with cybersex) is that the more you talk to them, the more you just want to be next to them or be in their arms.' Yet it was cybersex that taught her the wider dimensions to intimacy, a lesson she wants to retain, 'and it just kinda made me more free to open up to talk to people because you're on webcam, so you can't just sit and watch the person, you have to make conversation, and before I just used to smile and nod my head and now I just learn to converse'. As for her Jamaican partner, she found a way to transform things into what she hopes will become a long-term just-good-friends relationship. She simply turned off the webcam and now corresponds with him only by voice and through Facebook.

Stephanie

Webcam proved to be of huge importance to Stephanie, not just because she lost her virginity to webcam sex, but because webcam confirmed this as her primary relationship, and the one to which she remains committed. She had been friendly with Darren for quite some time before she went to Miami for her training as a nurse. While they were in Trinidad, there were always too many people around when they visited each other's house, and although they had fooled around a bit, nothing much had happened. In Miami, she found a different world. Whereas when living with an extended family in Trinidad, she was almost never alone, in Miami, Americans seemed to expect her to be entirely alone in her flat for long periods of time. Soon, she was not just alone, but lonely. Not wanting this to be evident to her family, who were paying for her training, she started to constantly Skype Darren, who was at that time about the only person on her Skype list, apart from her brother. This was where they learnt to sleep together in both senses. She would have her laptop on the pillow next to her. They used this even to establish who would routinely sleep on the right side of the bed and who on the left. If he didn't turn it off at night, it might still be there when she woke in the morning.

Skype was where they learnt how to live together. This way, Darren could get used to the idea that Stephanie could end the day coming home from training and just rant, to just need to get things off her chest, allowing the less extrovert Darren to help her regain her equanimity. Sometimes she just needed to argue, sometimes to hug and kiss through the webcam, sometimes to have a good cry, sometimes to eat together, or at least bring her meal to the camera. Sometimes, she just needed that they talk and talk and talk. Always-on allowed them to get used to living together. Maybe watching television, or getting changed, with the other there in the background. By the time she returned to Trinidad, they were an established couple. The visual aspect was hugely important, 'just being able to see how the face changes, that you got a new haircut, to see what you're wearing today – so I could say "you were wearing that yesterday, what you doing wearing that shirt again today?" The always-on element also added that major point of relaxation, which is simply not having to talk when you don't feel like it.' Similarly, she could manipulate the devices emotionally, turning off the visual when angry or because she didn't want to see him crying, though these periods of visual absence rarely lasted long, since they both craved the sight of each other.

It was on the basis of this increased intimacy that she in effect lost her virginity to Darren, and allowed webcam to establish the norms and routines for sex. This proved both ambiguous and asymmetrical. On the one hand, it seemed that he was controlling the action, doing very little himself but constantly suggesting this or that move to her – put the camera higher, move it out of focus and back again, which of them should climax first, or have a shower. And yet, to her own surprise, she experienced this as a manifestation of her control, even of her own selfishness, because in truth, she was not particularly turned on by anything Darren might do on camera: 'there is no eye candy for me on Skype'; rather she was turned on by the feeling of being watched and her actions. She felt it was she who was exploiting his gaze to achieve all sorts of erotic possibilities. She needed his commentary and appreciation, and indeed if she did most of the moving, he was doing most of the talking. This imbalance has been maintained since they met up and allowed co-present sex to take up the momentum. She thinks that webcam allows women to be selfish. She says that if it is true that men want to look, it is even more true that women want to be looked at.

Her problem with webcam came through an equally unanticipated consequence of the role of fantasy in this sexual exchange. It is hard to control what happens in your head, and for whatever reason, she couldn't stop herself thinking about the potential for her parents to see what she was doing. Although she took considerable precautions to make sure there was no recording of these webcam sessions, her enjoyment was clouded by this abiding sense of parental disapproval – sometimes her mother and sometimes her father. This seems to have been a factor in determining her behaviour when she returned to Trinidad. It seemed important now to become both upfront and strong-willed in having her parents come to terms with her being sexually active with Darren. The other slightly disturbing consequence was simply acknowledging knowing that being watched masturbating was a leitmotif of pornography. Although, this was not necessarily a bad thing, 'because the porn thing is definitely in your mind to the point where it would happen faster and more effectively for me, if I feel like I am looking like that'.

Donovan

As a Trinidadian man, Donovan confirms this experience of gendered asymmetry. 'The guy doesn't feel the kind of, he doesn't feel incumbent upon him to pretty up himself as much as the woman would. I mean I literally did nothing. I literally just took off my clothes, and laid on the bed and . . . Most of the time I was required to be the watcher really.' It was the women who focused upon appearance and the performance of themselves as alluring sensual bodies. Often, with considerable time and effort, he expanded on what clothes to put on and how to take them off. Donovan's job was to provide the intense interest evident in detailed instructions and suggestions. In fact, Donovan admitted that sometimes he was actually not really in the mood, but it was essential to at least feign interest, otherwise the woman who was conducting her elaborate performance might become quite upset at this lack of appreciation. His role was to instruct: 'Well, at least from my point of view. I mean, you're giving them a script.' Rather than faking orgasm, Donovan found himself to be the fake voyeur.

Perhaps this was why Donovan eventually felt ready for something entirely different. For many men, and Donovan seems typical in this regard, there is a kind of dualism to webcam sex. On the one hand, this tends to start as another arena of pleasure, an entertaining space of exploration and play with any woman who will agree to become one's erotic interlocutor. Yet, for a committed long-term relationship, this needs to transform into something altogether different and serious. In particular, a person one respects as one's wife needs to be lifted out from that morass of inconsequential erotic encounters, and to become an object of a very different kind of idealized fantasy. This is a theme of Miller's previous work on what he called the mutual antagonism of sexuality and property in Trinidad (1994: 193–201). His account included the example of men who were impotent with their wives, but not with their *deputies* (mistresses), because of this need to separate out the role of wife from sexual promiscuity. Donovan, therefore, would not be unusual in creating a profound contrast between the description of his webcam relationship to the woman who is now his wife, and to all those other women he had had relationships with online.

Although they had seen each other offline, it was through webcam that Donovan really came to know his wife. It was most definitely a meeting of minds rather than bodies, a genuine interest in all other aspects of this person. They subsequently developed an offline physical relationship. Yet, online engagement only achieved the depth and richness of their offline life when his wife became pregnant. This was when his sense of loss in being physically separated combined with the desperate need to see her body and for her to be seen, making webcam central to everything. 'I mean, like when she got VERY pregnant, I'd see him kicking and all the goings on . . . all these little things, and just comfort. That time, is a very emotional time for these things, I mean, she needs some kind of comfort. She would need to see me . . . She actually got very impatient with the whole MSN thing by the time she got pregnant so it was very much a Skype business.' By this time, we are very far from Donovan's previously indifferent attitude to his role in casual webcam sex. He is passionate about seeing his pregnant wife. In his own way, Donovan seems to have thereby learnt just as much as Shantel, through the experience of webcam, about the wider contexts to physical relationships.

Trinidadians are not particularly reticent about pornography, but, as with homosexuality, it is something one would have to focus on if we wanted to talk about it with any authority. Our research was insufficient in that regard. It was not in Trinidad but in our earlier pilot study in London that we encountered Tonia, who in a series of discussions developed a theme which gives us a rather more profound view of how webcam sex can be transformative in the life of an individual. By ending with Tonia, we can also start to generalize beyond the Trinidadian context to consider webcam, intimacy and sex more widely.

Tonia

Another advantage of ending with Tonia is that she was more direct than most about the issues of technology and emotion that are central to our theory of attainment. Hers is a story of webcam as redemption, an instrument that brings Tonia back to life in certain respects and so, as in the theory of attainment, shows the role of technology in constituting rather than detracting from humanity. But, there is one more final reason for ending with Tonia, which was her own insistence that if we were working with her, then her stipulated condition was that we would publish her story, because she felt people have so much to learn from it.

The starting point of her narrative has to be in her childhood, when Tonia was sexually abused by her step-father. She was old enough for this to have huge implications for her emergent (mis) understanding of sexuality itself. She, like others, came to view herself as damaged in that regard, as having experienced something that might for ever have stymied her potential for linking sex with intimacy. Born in one of the more difficult areas of London, she'd had a rough life. For several years, she was a drug dealer, which led to her own desperate need for rehab. From early on, she was no stranger to online pornography and her interest in cybersex developed in part from her ambivalence about one of her longer term relationships, where it had become clear that her boyfriend had no qualms about carrying on cybersex relationships, entirely separately from his relationship with her.

Her own initial online sexual experiences were without webcam. She became adept at building up the erotic tension with a mixture of voice, instant messaging or in photos. 'It becomes very clear, it becomes very explicit, enticing, you're asking for certain things, you become very demanding, you say what's kind of happening in your body. So it's pretty full on when it's got to this stage. It could be, you know, "I'm wet, I'm throbbing, I'm hot, I'm this, I'm that, I'm gonna remove". It could be that sort of thing. It could be "I'm thinking about such and such, sharing something you've said, something you've seen . . . telling a story". The scope is huge.'

She was always cautious about webcam, aware of the dangers of someone recording and then broadcasting the results to others. She was very careful about showing her face. But gradually, webcam became integral to the wider experience of cybersex:

> The majority of people would have more than one webcam. They set up a space for it, that's my experience. I was different in that, because I would take my laptop to different rooms. I quite enjoyed that side of things, particularly my bathroom, which kind of seemed like fun and different and atmosphere, light and steam and all that. I'm just a creative person! I'd set things up properly, I'd have mini tables and things, and that could be quite fun. You'd be flexible in the way you'd be doing things and was enjoyable from that point of view – staging and having props to stage and that encouraged thinking about it later and the imagination.

Tonia emphasized the importance of this phase of online sexuality to her own sexual healing. In this, she certainly does not romanticize her own role. The sense one gets from her description is that, at least early on, she could be very cold, manipulative, demanding and cynical; sometimes enjoying the degree to which she might make a fool of, or humiliate, a correspondent. But this reflected the hurt she had suffered, and what mattered is that gradually things could improve and become healthier on both sides.

> Because we're talking directly about sex here right; I think the single mindedness, is a quality to it, i.e. to be seen, genitally, erotically. There is no other focus other than that: the beauty, the

> gorgeousness, the attractiveness, the lusciousness, the desire for that. So the rest of the life which may be completely fragmented, maybe no status, maybe feeling low esteemed in certain areas in their lives, that doesn't come into it. Whereas in the social scenario, hell yeah, the fact that you are in a certain pub, a certain restaurant, whatever, would be indicators to who you are, what clothes you wear, it would be all those signatures imprinted. Whereas the webcam side, you are just seen, and you only want to be seen, then you can be seen in that attractiveness just as you are in the rawest sense.
>
> Ultimately it's about how I can intensely look at my own body. One of the features about abuse is to separate from your own body, to trip out of your own body, you can become disembodied in that way, detached from it. So in webcam, part of it is to go – this is my breast, this is my skin, this is my leg, these are my lips, this is mine, to be able to say I'm revealing this, there is a healing in that, I'm owning this body. But you've got to present it. It's not only about what you see, but what I give you to see, what I reveal to you. So a performance, what you reveal, that's the key healing part.

Tonia gives many details of this process of healing. For example, she gives an important insight into the way the concept of a computer crashing becomes integral to people's wider sense of emotional vulnerability in such sexual exchanges:

> There was just this thing about crashing that I wanted to come back to. The crash side, I think people crash for a number of reasons. They lose confidence, they feel excluded, they might not have the language to know how to interact in that situation when it takes an unexpected turn. They feel offended by something that is said, and of course there is the environmental. The kids have just woken up, someone's just come back from work, the phone's gone and they can see oh my God this is an important call, I've got to take it, and rather than navigate around any of that – off. People can just abandon ship, switch off. So apart from the computer crash, it's an emotional crash, where you didn't get your closure or your climax and you don't know what state you're in.
>
> That point needs to be seriously emphasized in this whole self care thing, handling being abandoned in the middle of an interaction is a big deal. If you've been building your confidence and that's one of the ways you're building your confidence, you might not have the language to say that's what you're doing, but in effect that's what you are doing. Then suddenly, somebody just

> disappears and you can see they're not trying to get back to you. The technology is such that you can see when somebody's trying to get back to you. Then that's different, because you know they're trying to reach you. But if this person is not, and there is no text to say why this person is not happening, then that can be harsh, it can sit harshly. So managing the crash and understanding crashes, and bear in mind that some people even get embittered by crashes and they get stung by them and as a result the relationships with other people online changes. So whereas before they might have had a bit of etiquette, they would follow up and all of that, and I've done that myself.

This is not, then, a story of simple cathartic redemption. What Tonia shows is that coming back into control of one's own sexuality through webcam is difficult and has its own dangers and pitfalls. Even in this de-contextualized sexual interaction, outside of the expected intimacy of a more sustained relationship, there are emotional investments and dangers. But for all that, Tonia was clear that ultimately, this was her means for successfully overcoming her own detachment from sexuality that derived from the initial abuse. This media and the degree to which webcam allowed her a greater measure of control than face-to-face sex was her mode of self-healing and progression.

> *[And can one say, that the relationships you've had since then were better?]* Sexually, yes. And primarily because the language had improved, and the areas I'd say that it had improved on in my life was: one – I discovered language and fantasies that I hadn't thought about, that I enjoyed and the language for that. And two – there was greater fluency in talking about sex. And three – the realism, it helped me to be more real in some ways, and this is related to the crash point. It helped me to demystify sex. I had had two extremes, either violence or the walls. My relationship would lead to happily ever after, all healing, all tender all sensual, all adoring, where we would have lots of children, *Little House on the Prairie* style. So it would either be that, or there was violence or some kind of cruelty and abandonment and all that kind of stuff. So it was very rarely anything in between. One of the things that whole world introduced to me was that there was a whole spectrum of interactions that go on in the world, and there actually can be a lot of respect around it too. And that I found fascinated me, discovering that.

> And also, I would like to emphasize the point about women's fluency to talk about sex as well. I think it's important to emphasize as well. Otherwise the study would be male dominated. It's all pretty clear what we're all fucking there for. We're all there to explore sex in some shape or form, and at last, and there's often about the advice giving that's going on in there, about different things, different interactions, watch out for this, watch out for that, places to go, check this, check that. Watch out for this person, fantasies, ideas. There was a liberation for discussion between women, and that should not be underestimated in this, me thinks. And I'll be very disappointed if I don't see that in your study! I will look out for that!

Conclusion

In Chapter Two, we emphasized the importance of specific cultural genres from Trinidad. This will remain significant throughout this volume, but anthropologists today need to also work with wider spheres. Tonia may be born in the UK, but the world of online pornography is global and, mostly, she would not even know where in the world her interlocutors were located. In this conclusion we are then looking at a wider, more general sphere. We have traversed a world of intimacy, starting with the impact of an increasingly global discourse of romance to end with a case that is anything but romantic. The central point that emerges from Tonia's story is congruent with much of the rest of this chapter, including the sections on non-sexual intimacy. Not everyone takes to webcam or finds it comfortable. Equally, there are many cases where people feel awkward, pressured and uncomfortable in co-present interactions. As people's experience of webcam develops, they start to explore areas where webcam can help them to overcome the limitations of co-presence, or allow them, as in the case of Tonia, to progress in an area of sex or intimacy, which might not have been possible in co-present relationships. We started by seeing webcam as a partial solution to the problem of separation and absence. Then gradually we come to appreciate that webcam is not merely the *other* to co-presence, but is its own sphere of intimate relationships. In some cases, it may become fully constitutive of relationships. The point is not to be judgemental with regard to webcam as positive or negative, a better or worse approximation to something else. As it develops, webcam will lead to quite unprecedented genres of sort-of-co-presence that transcend mere comparison with these prior forms.

At the start of this chapter, we returned to one of the major arguments within our theory of attainment, which is that new digital media should be used to expose the mediated nature of offline communication, rather than, as is common to much writing on digital culture, to reinforce the illusion that face-to-face represented previously unmediated authenticity. One might think of sex as the epitome of the intrinsically co-present relationship. Then we read about Shantel and we remember that having sex is not of itself sufficient for most people to constitute a relationship; with webcam, her boyfriend actually had to talk to her; clearly her co-present partners had rarely paid her that courtesy.

Kaufmann (2012) has studied online sex as principally something that takes sex out of context. We also found instances of this. There is a specifically Trinidadian website that is today mainly populated by explicit photos and videos of ex-girlfriends in the act of sex. They are almost certainly posted without their permission, and very likely including underage schoolgirls. Even more problematic is that these sites often appear to state at least the general area in which these girls live. We differ from Kaufmann in seeing many examples of the opposite, where for Shantel, it was offline sex that had routinely been reduced to the merely physical. Even for Tonia, who does engage in de-contextualized webcam sex, Skype allowed her to re-configure the wider contours of mutual respect and self-respect that healed her previous damaged relationship to sex itself.

We learn more by examining sex within the context of insights gained through the study of non-erotic intimacy, as between parents and children as well as separated couples. If we focus upon sex, then intimacy is equated with moments of intense concentration on the other person. This chapter showed how the opposite can be true. The reason why always-on webcam is growing in importance is that it exposes the way that in-your-face mode of webcam as videophone often fails to convey intimacy through intensity. Instead, it is only when webcam recreates the domestic conditions within which you can now take the other person for granted, where there is no pressure to communicate at all, that we feel a more complete sense of intimacy. This may have been true throughout the history of co-residence, but always-on webcam makes one aware of and sensitive to how intimacy operated offline. We thereby come to appreciate that while we benefit from Goffman's study of public encounters, we have so far failed to expose the analogous forms of subtle cultural mediation that have allowed us to cohabit within this very private world.

A theory of attainment doesn't mean that we are always looking for something that is newly achieved. Quite the contrary, it is much more about using the study of technology to come to appreciate what has already been attained. It refuses to regard technology as increased mediation or approximations to some precedent. Instead, we have used this chapter for a detailed investigation of what we mean by the very term intimacy, often without realizing it. Webcam has exposed the routines, presumptions and hidden collusions that have always allowed us to live together. The delicious irony of webcam is that in some areas it most effectively establishes intimacy when we stop using it to communicate and attain the nirvana of a relaxed love or sufficiency of autonomy that doesn't have to constantly express itself.

4

The Sense of Place

Living inside the web

Much of the academic interest in new communication technologies, especially that of social scientists, has concentrated on usage by diasporic migrants (recent examples include Fortunati et al., 2012; Greschke, 2012; Madianou and Miller, 2012a). This is a natural focus of analysis, which also accorded with what users saw as common sense. In a world in which a global political economy is creating demands for mass migration and an increase in transnational work, we would want to understand the potential of new media for re-connecting people living in conditions of separation. Miller's 2011 study of Facebook suggested, however, an alternative way of conceptualizing these media. Instead of thinking about them as instruments which connect separate locations, we may have reached the point where we should start to think of new media as places in which people in some sense live; a third place, distinct from the two offline locations. Three factors contributed to this radical re-thinking of the relationship between media and place. The first was that with mobile smartphones, it was no longer the case that specific location was of particular consequence. It no longer really mattered where a person and their phone was, as the connection between people was through the medium of the phone itself, in which they were temporarily within the same communicative space, rather than being connected as otherwise located persons.

The second point was that people in Facebook spent a considerable amount of time working on the look and style of their appearance online, as had perhaps been even more the case with MySpace. Horst (2009) had shown how an aesthetic concern with the appearance of their online location could be directly linked with an equal concern for the aesthetics of the bedrooms of the teenagers she had studied in California. Sometimes, the online style was designed to match the look of the bedroom in which the computer was situated. The question is often raised as to why people spend so much time cultivating the appearance of their online sites with photos and other paraphernalia. We are often told that being online is making us more superficial or trivial. If instead of seeing Facebook as merely a mode of communication, it was designated as the place in which you lived, then this transforms our perception of such activity into another example of home decoration, which makes it much less strange and more amenable to conventional analysis. People are not dismissed as trivial because they pay attention to the furnishing and decoration of their homes.

The third factor comes not from Facebook, but from webcam itself, where the phenomenon we describe in the last chapter as 'always-on' has the clear accoutrements of people living together in the same space, mimicking the taken for grantedness of domestic co-presence. Here, the conjuncture of space is created by webcam itself. All three of these observations may be reinforced by the more general observation with regard to Facebook that it was people whose location was constrained, such as Dr Karamath, who couldn't leave his house for reasons of illness, who, in effect, lived all day on, and perhaps we can now say within, Facebook (Miller, 2011).

It would be simplest to proclaim this as a Copernican shift in our perception from seeing communication as that which links between locations to seeing it as a place in its own right. However, what this would do is merely confirm a prior period as the stable moment of taken-for-granted domestic co-present location, which is now disrupted by this extraordinary new possibility of being located outside of location. As anthropologists, however, we should always see this from the other end of the telescope. This appreciation that people don't need to be located in households should remind us that comparative studies, central to anthropology, would in any case have revealed a far more diverse set of potential relationships to location than the now conventional domestic residence. As traditional studies of the household noted, there were always diverse configurations of the triangle between house, family and household, ranging from tribal collective men's houses to homes which did not assume kin relations between occupants (Wilk, 1989). Even in countries such as Canada, Norway and the UK, amongst ordinary suburban populations, the relationship to the home as location is much more dynamic and diverse than is usually acknowledged (Clarke, 2001; Garvey, 2001; Marcoux, 2001). It is also well established that media have an important bearing on the way people understand both their concept of home (see Morley, 2000 for an extensive discussion) and their sense of homeland (see Basu, 2007). We might therefore welcome the way the study of new media returns anthropology to this much broader and earlier anthropological understanding, rescuing us from the parochial assumptions of the house as domestic home for the nuclear family, which in many regions is largely the product of relatively recent ideology and governance (Hayden, 1981).

In this chapter, we will explore these issues in stages. First, we will look at how webcam destabilizes the assumptions we have about the presence of the person. Then we will see how it may destabilize the concept of home. We will then look at the more general relationship to the place where we live. We will briefly consider the location of the computer itself, before finally turning to look at the re-stabilization of location for those living abroad.

Attention

The previous chapter emphasized the positive potential of digital anthropology in drawing our attention to norms of pre-digital communication that had been taken for granted. We want to suggest that the issue of paying *attention* is one of these. In her recent book, Broadbent (2011) makes this term central to her documentation of the changing relationship between work and non-work resulting from increasing communications between the two spheres. She argues that one of the main reasons for the success of media such as Facebook is that they are relatively undemanding of attention. One can respond at one's leisure, contrasted with the compulsion posed by a ringing phone that demands immediate attention.

Our participants highlighted another dimension of attention: the fear of whether one's correspondent is actually paying attention to this act of communication. This is nothing new. To give two classic examples – everyone has been at a party and felt that the self-important person they were speaking to was not really listening to a word we were saying because they were more focused on gazing around the room, looking for someone of greater consequence they would prefer to be talking to. Similarly, there are many films with scenes of a quarrel within a marriage in which one partner says to the other that although they constantly talk, the other partner never actually listens to what they have been saying, and hasn't done so for years.

Both of these examples imply a serious breakdown from the normative expectation of everyday conversation, where attention is presumed. The evidence from our webcam study suggests that new communication media have created a genuine break from that normative condition, in that it is now possible to be simultaneously and surreptitiously engaged in another conversation. It is this disparity between presence and attention that is creating a new anxiety. In the Philippines, it is quite common for a person to be talking to you and at the same time texting with someone else. People are so adept at texting, they don't need to be looking at their phones. Their mouth is talking to one person, while their fingers are talking to another. On Facebook, many Trinidadians engage in multiple, often six or more, chat conversations at the same time.

The fear of rivals for attention pertains to more than other conversations. It may be a concern that one's correspondent is playing a computer game, doing some work, watching the news, or in some other way not really there. Webcam can equally exacerbate such anxiety because you can be doing other things, or alleviate it when you can see whether someone is doing other things. The consequence we can observe is that today, unlike our two previous examples of rudeness, webcam has made this issue of attention become an integral part of relationships rather than necessarily a sign of relationship break down. Once again we have an ever present issue regarding what it means for someone to be present, but now brought to the foreground of our own academic attention.

Some new media are helping resolve, while others exemplify, these issues. It was with the conventional phone that you called without knowing what situation you might be thereby interrupting. Today, people often text first to check if the phone call is convenient. By contrast, some new media are even more compulsive than the ringing phone. Many Trinidadians suggested that the BlackBerry was particularly problematic, since incoming BBM messages can be a constant throughout the day and elicited a response that seemed close to addiction:

> They hear that 'beep beep beep' and they just send their message even while they're speaking to you. 'Beep beep beep' and out goes the phone and it has to be 'and what were you saying again?' Kara readily admits that when talking to her husband, 'Yeah but I'd probably be texting somebody else, like a friend, you know, like if somebody's BBMing me, I can text and talk to him yeah, like if my friend pops up and ask a question. I can do that while talking to him because it's, you know. But he knows, because I think he probably feels that if we're having a conversation, BBM should not interrupt. He probably is not as BBM savvy as I am.

This takes us back to the distinctions between webcam as videophone and webcam as always-on in Chapter Three. Some see visibility as an assurance of attention. They use it to sit and stare at each other throughout the call, regarding any extraneous activity as a betrayal. In this example, one can see how this comes to connote also the intensity of sexual attention:

> The funny part is that when she moved back to Trinidad, we broke up, we didn't see eye to eye. And that was pretty strange, we got so accustomed – this is my theory – we got so accustomed to the webcam stuff and I put 'stuff' in inverted commas, that when she came back home, we didn't . . . do stuff anymore. She was here for a year and that entire year things declined drastically and we broke up, and that's why I have a new girlfriend now.

Sometimes the degree of undivided attention is inferred to be a cultural or gender trait; 'I'm not a woman. I can't do two things at once you know. I've gotta sit there and talk to her, you know, but I can't be doing other stuff. You know us men, we can't concentrate. So yeah, I just sit there and face to face talk.' It was more common to assume that it is women who are demanding of undivided attention as a sign of commitment:

> There are times where my husband is multi-tasking and I find it rude, and I have told him that, I recognize though that when my husband speaks, he's like playing on the computer, yes the video image is there, but he is not necessarily interacting with the image unless my son is there, then yes he's interacting, but with me, it's not as if he's looking the entire time. He multi-tasks.

The use of webcam to check on the degree of attention was predictable. Less expected was the way it facilitated a movement away from such surveillance, especially for younger people. One explanation is given by Leanda, a teenager, the group for whom this multi-tasking is most evident:

> Yeah because you know when you're on the phone, you have to have the phone at your ear all the time, you can't really do other stuff, so like if I'm on the webcam talking to somebody I could do schoolwork, I could study, I could be folding clothes, because my hands are free, yeah, I'll still be speaking to them. Well I might be on Facebook while I'm on Skype, or I might be reading a book, studying, while I'm on Skype. I tend not to play games while I'm on Skype, I don't think my computer could do that, it'd probably slow it down. Well if I'm up late on the computer studying, well the person in Trinidad, I'd probably call them and so we'd both be doing work but generally like probably every ten minutes we'll talk for a while, and then get back to work. But my friends abroad, I just call them to actually talk.

It is likely that these early experiences of webcam are a transient phase during which people don't quite know how to interpret each other's actions. One can see this ambivalence in the following discussion:

> Actually that was kinda odd because like when you're speaking to someone face to face in person, you know you could do other stuff while talking to them. But like using the webcam, it's kinda hard at first, because you call them for a purpose, so you'd expect, you know. On the phone, it's undivided attention, they're speaking to you all the time, it's not like that on a webcam, it's not like they will be talking to you all the time, they'll be doing other stuff as well.

Meanwhile, some people manipulate or just have fun with these ambiguities. A Brazilian noted:

> When he's watching a soccer game I'm like 'look, I'm not going to fight with soccer or cars, it's OK, we can talk later but don't give me this mediocre attention business.' And sometimes he gets really annoyed as well, like if I start reading an e-mail, Oh he gets really jealous if there is multi-media talking. Like when I'm talking to someone on Skype but there is also the Skype message open, he always says, 'Who are you talking to? Pay attention to me!' like he gets really really upset. Like you think you can multi-task, you can't, especially because he is seeing me, if he is not seeing me I can get away with it. But you know he can tell because I'm like 'ummm, mmmmm', and then he says 'You're not paying attention to me.' And by the third time he says that, I have to close all of the other things. Or, tell him 'you know what? I'm actually really enjoying my other conversation with my best friend, who is in New York, and I haven't talked to her, so I will hang up with you and call you later.' And then he says 'thank you – I would rather you do that then dilly dally your attention in three other places'. And then sometimes I catch him on his sport pages on his iPad.

Presence used to be assumed, unless someone was being rude or inconsiderate. On the phone, one didn't worry partly because one didn't really know if people were otherwise engaged. Webcam seems to have de-stabilized these assumptions around attention. Teenagers may be quite comfortable with the discrepancy between presence and attention, couples may play with it, but, more often, people are unsettled by it. The contribution to the wider concerns of this chapter is the way webcam leads to a much more open debate as to what location actually means and where these people are best described as being during their conversations, and thereby questions the very nature of presence and location.

De-stabilizing the home

The issue of attention shows how webcam is de-stabilizing norms around being present. Alongside always-on webcam, the idea that we might be living in some way within the media in turn de-stabilizes the idea and ideal of domestic life. There are good precedents to this. The most unequivocal adulation for the home as a site of domesticity in the 1950s came just before the feminist revolution and re-marking of the domestic as a form of gender oppression, hiding modes of exploitation. A recent paper by the geographer Katherine Brickell (2011), based on her studies of divorce and separation in Cambodia, includes a useful bibliography of studies showing how the ideology of the home has papered over many cracks, including domestic conflicts and contradictions between household members, requiring, she argues, a more critical geography. We need these reminders that the nuclear family home is a specific cultural norm based on ideology not a psychological given. At the same time, we recognize that this model of domestic bliss is now a pervasive and accepted condition for many of our informants, which leads them to experience new media as a disruption to the normal order of the world.

When the personal computer first went on sale, most families could only afford a single computer. Lally (2002) examined the subsequent arguments over who had use and control over that machine, comparing these with more traditional ideas of property rights and conflicted ownership. More recently, there has been a spate of research on youth and new media, for example, Ito (2009), Livingstone and Haddon (2009) and boyd (2013). As teenagers gain access to computers in their own room, parents may almost palpably feel that their children have stopped living in their home, but rather, as in *The Lion, The Witch and the Wardrobe* (Lewis, 1950), the computer has become a portal that allows their children to escape the confines of their bedrooms and live in some other world entirely. An extreme version of these contradictions was evident in an excellent MSc thesis by Penni Fu, a student in the UCL Digital Anthropology programme, looking at the impact of computers upon urban children in China (2010). As a result of the one child per family policy, parents feel huge pressures to see the computer as facilitating the education of their children. For urban Chinese, education is of immense importance. As a result, they tend to repress the evidence that this is the machine that gives those same children the means to escape from these educational pressures within the privacy of their own rooms.

This is one of many ways in which media technologies are experienced as de-stabilizing the home. Sometimes the problem is not change but stasis that creates a sense of existential unease.

Gilsenan (2005) once pointed out that when cities such as New Delhi or New Cairo were created, other people found themselves designated as Old Delhi or Old Cairo, often against their will. They have not changed anything, but the rise of the new has re-designated who they are. An insightful recent book by Chu (2010) looks at the impact of outward migration in a region of China, in making those who remain feel antiquated and neglected. In our work, it was not uncommon, especially for older people, to feel they had no choice but to embrace webcam, even if they didn't particularly want to, as either they would be left out and rendered even more isolated, or they would have a new form of dependency upon their more technologically adept younger relatives, which in some cases they resented. Their domestic worlds have been de-stabilized by webcam, because to remain unchanged is no longer a stable state.

In their work on the Philippines, Madianou and Miller (2012a) found a very different de-stabilization as a result of improved communications. Most of the absentee Filipina mothers felt that being able to communicate with their children so readily and so often meant they were able to recapture their sense of being a mother. Yet, the authors also found that the children could be much more ambivalent. One reason was that a child with an absent mother can control their own often idealized representation of their mother as the figure of love and comfort as they require. With new media, they are much more in touch with their actual mothers, who sometimes seem quite distant from this ideal. They are now aware of how their mother constantly tries to imagine the children as younger than they actually are, or how they use the new media for extreme surveillance that fails to recognize the autonomy that the children have now achieved. New media exposes the discrepancy between the idealized mother and the person they now have to contend with many times a day. As a result, the concept of 'mother' is de-stabilized rather than recaptured. Once again, a central foundation to the domestic idyll is rendered problematic by new media.

In a similar way, webcam can be said to increase homesickness. Individuals may strive to become reconciled to absence, so that they can achieve a gradual adaptation to their new environment. Prior media such as phone conversations were less disturbing of this process, but the intensely personal and visual contact facilitated by webcam could make it highly disruptive of this gradual settling in. People talked as though they had suffered a relapse back to a less reconciled state. 'Yes. Um, sometimes I do definitely have that feeling of "OK, the Skype conversation is over, I'm suddenly not there anymore." It's kind of hard because you have to reconnect with reality, and the reality of the distance. So I do find it hard, sometimes I do find it lonelier, even though I am surrounded by people.' Another person once made a *callaloo* (the Trinidadian national dish made of a leafy vegetable, locally called dasheen bush) to show her relative abroad, but having seen the reaction, decided never to do so again. The visual evidence of home cooking was particularly disturbing. A Trini woman noted:

> I think it definitely made me homesick when I saw sort of my mom sitting in her desk and then in the background is you know the living room at home with the TV . . . you know the books along the wall and I actually, I know exactly where things are, and you know I go in there, sometimes I feel like I can crawl into the webcam into the computer screen and into the room and be at home for a little bit you know so it made me sort of homesick in that sense, but it also made me less homesick because I can actually see my parents and know that they're okay.

Others may feel that webcam obviates the need to establish any kind of reconciliation with the new physical location. There are Filipina women in London who have almost no relationship to London itself – they never eat out, go to the cinema or to a pub. Their lives are split between socializing with other Filipina women in London, but increasingly living their non-working hours online and webcamming with their friends and relatives within the Philippines. One may say they work in London, or sleep in London, but it is not clear any more that they live in London. Similarly, a Trini talks of her sister in Texas living on a US military base with no close friends there at all. Her social life remains essentially her connections with her family back in Trinidad, which are maintained through Skype. In the case of some cousins, she has never seen them in the flesh, but feels that Skype is sufficient to constitute a more meaningful relationship with them than anyone she knows on the military base. She says that on the base, there are few black people, and her child was quite upset by a racist remark when she went shopping, and whenever she has a problem or feels lonely, she returns to the potential for Skyping with Trinidad.

A final example, which arose only a few times in our fieldwork, is that of people who webcam each other from within the same house. Just as when workers first started emailing between offices in the same building, this seems to shock people who hear of the practice as though it is a failure to acknowledge proximity. One person was indignant about the very idea of it. They called this a waste of webcam, a thoroughly pointless and unnecessary exercise. People seem upset by the way this questions the presumed sociality of cohabitation. As a result, a Trini who does this regularly felt the need to justify herself. She noted that she has a hectic work schedule and may not return home till late evening. Her brother will be in his room doing his own thing and she doesn't want to disturb him. But when she turns on her computer and sees her brother online, it seems natural to then have a webcam chat about whatever has been going on in the day, problems or successes at work and so forth. Webcam also resolves the common problem of what to do about closed doors within your own house and not knowing if it's a good time to knock. Sometimes, the grounds are simple logistics. A woman who is living in a converted garage Skypes her mother to check on the cooking in the kitchen and asks her to turn the oven up or down. All of which suggests that one day, internal domestic webcamming, texting and Facebook messaging will become just as acceptable as inter-office emailing. Yet, these same people still regarded face to face as preferable for discussing significant issues such as an illness in the family.

Establishing location

All the above examples suggest that webcam, along with other new media, can be experienced as a threat to the ideal of the domestic. It is not surprising, then, that we find many ways in which these same technologies are used to re-establish location. When mobile phones first became popular, people felt the first thing they needed to do was let the other person know where they were irrespective of whether location was relevant to the conversation. This varies with respect to webcam. In certain cases, such as a boyfriend insisting on seeing the surroundings of his girlfriend, there are clear connotations of surveillance and jealousy, and similarly when a woman checks whether a man is really in the library. Another reason for showing location is to celebrate it, pointing the webcam at ornaments or more commonly the garden. Martin uses webcam to take people around what he regards as his estate with his favourite fruit trees, as well as showing the people back home the fancy hotel he was staying in while on holiday abroad; though Trinidadians, who are generally more egalitarian than most, have to couch such showing off with humour or banter to make such behaviour acceptable.

For Trinidadians, the home they are reasserting can often be Trinidad itself. When the internet first developed (Miller and Slater, 2000: 103–15), Trinis would devote themselves to creating websites in which they anonymously took on the task of presenting key national emblems such as the flag or the best beaches, so webcam may be used to show an aspect of Carnival or lush tropical vegetation, an extension of the very strong sense of national pride that is conspicuous in Trinidad. Similarly, today, a diasporic Trini may ask to see the town they have come from to catch up on all the latest developments, such as the new fire station, or whether their school has changed much.

People can also be conscious of the position of the webcam itself. As Anthony notes, 'Yeah so I try to clean up the surroundings because my grandmother is one to note 'Oh it's dirty there, go and clean up, sweep up' yeah, that's how she is.' Another Trini affirms that an untidy or dirty background can be left as long as one is talking to a close friend, similar to when a person is visiting. By contrast, Randy employs the mobility of a laptop to move Skype around from kitchen to backyard, according to whatever he happens to be doing. English male informants may have a small but significant vision of paradise consisting of lying in bed, webcamming through a laptop resting on one's belly, with crisps within reach of one hand and a can of beer within reach of the other.

Location becomes something of a more interesting problem when webcam becomes a virtual invitation of others into the bedroom, a place previously banned to all but very intimate friends. In general, it seemed that people either didn't want or didn't feel the need to see things this way, and were surprised when the analogy was suggested. Some feel that as long as one is decently covered, this signifies ease and comfort and is unproblematic. But one woman was surprised that her friend appeared entirely comfortable to be Skyping in her nightclothes. Another noted:

> I don't even think it's embarrassment, it's I . . . the word that comes to mind is protection. You can't, someone I've only just met, has no right to look in my home, yeah I don't know it's just harsh as that, like I've done a lot to protect my home and everything in it, including the children and stuff like that, and if some arsehole online is just not going to get to peer in . . . no, they will have to earn that right to come to my home. Because I'm complex and you know, you can't just sort of look at it and think you know what you're looking at, yeah?

For families who can afford only a single computer, there is also the issue of whether, like the TV, it will itself become a focus of family life and orientation. Turkle (2011) sees the TV as having established itself as part of a domestic setting for shared viewing, while the computer, although increasingly a portal for TV programmes and other entertainment, had for a while a more individualistic and excluding aura. This may be changing as young couples in London mostly watch TV through their computer and then webcam while sitting together as a couple, which probably portends a shift towards more socialized usage in the future. Our evidence is closer to Rainie and Wellman (2012), in seeing changes in the forms of sociality rather than the extent of sociality.

For those Trinis used to a bustling traditional household, webcamming is rarely a singular affair. They expect a constant stream of people intruding, either passing in the background, casually interrupting and taking part in a conversation, or young children complaining because they want to see the computer being used for something more enthralling. These Trinis do not assume some natural individualization around webcamming, because their home environment never had that sense of presumed autonomy. Webcam thereby brings the correspondent into the bosom of incessantly social family life. This thereby re-establishes a domestic idyll. But domestic life in El Mirador, with hardly any sense of privacy, bears no relation to the respect for order and autonomy that is seen as central to the cohabitation of families in the UK or

US. We have moved from attention to the person, to a wider relationship to the home and domestic life. Both were found to be disturbed and sometimes re-established through the advent of webcam. Certainly the technology has made us at least temporarily more conscious and self-conscious about our sense of place. This can also pertain to the larger context of place as in, for example, national identity or global citizenship. In this case we will make our arguments through contrastive stories that illustrate how people follow through some particular logic in creating their particular sense of place.

Jason and Nikhil

The case of Jason illustrates how the propensity to identify with the internet as a kind of place depends not just on this new relationship to the digital media, but just as much on one's previous sense of place and the degree to which their personal sense of identity was connected to location. Jason was not a Trinidadian, but from St Vincent, one of the smaller Caribbean islands. Not surprisingly, many people from these smaller Caribbean islands have a much more transnational sense of themselves as compared to Trinidadians who, Jason suggests, are often so obsessed with Trinidad that they barely acknowledge the wider Caribbean, except as a source of migration. Apart from this less parochial sense of place, there are additional reasons why Jason, in particular, would be less fixated on location or physical space. Jason's real interest in life is acting, but acting within art contexts including performance art, which is in some ways a double abstraction. One aspect is the self-consciousness of both himself and others as distanced from their apparent presence, because of the degree to which they are acting as themselves. For someone as academic as Jason, who likes to quote figures such as Judith Butler, there is also an analytical abstraction of separation from mere presence.

These kinds of involvement in the arts also tend to lead towards a positive identification with a cosmopolitanism that is in any case transnational. There may be only one or two other people in St Vincent who could in any way be seen as on the same wavelength in terms of Jason's particular and quite esoteric artistic sensibility. So even without the internet, he would be identifying with a more translocal set, who have gravitated towards this particular field of artistic practice. The affinity with the internet is very evident. From early on, the internet was viewed as a place where people with very particular hobbies, interests or beliefs could form transnational networks that were based on common identity of interest as opposed to mere physical location. Jason was now living in Trinidad, but would be in regular webcam contact with people all over the world, including practitioners of this variety of performance art in Japan or Argentina, who are using Skype to manifest their relationship to acting. Jason will look up key figures in his movement and make contact directly. For such performance artists, individuals come into being through being seen by those who are able to appreciate them as embodied performance; a person is created as artefact rather than a given authenticity. Authenticity is, rather, something they achieve through the vision of the other (see Kirshenblatt-Gimblett, 1998). This is an extreme example of observations we made in earlier chapters about the Trinidadian concept of the self, the difference being that, for these performance artists, only a knowledgeable and appreciative eye viewing them is real. That eye can see them even through webcam, contrasted with an ignorant eye that may well be in the same room but cannot actually see them. It therefore seems particularly reasonable to envisage someone like Jason as not just living on webcam, but coming alive in that presence, in a way that may be harder to manifest offline.

Nikhil is in several ways the opposite of Jason. Nikhil has a strong sense of identity centred around the idea that he is an authentic Trinidadian residing in Trinidad. Miller and Slater (2000: 103–15) argued that when the internet first came to Trinidad, the result was not the expected blurring of geography. Rather, it was an acute consciousness of the specificity of being Trinidadian, in response to the realization that most of the world has barely heard of them. Nikhil loves to see himself as an ambassador for Trinidad, but the point is not, as it might have been for others, that he puts himself forward as an exemplary Trini. For him, being an ambassador consists of being the conduit that brings others to a proper appreciation of Trinidad, rather than of him personally. The key advantage of webcam is simply that he can directly present Trinidad to these others. To be born Trini is a blessing of fate to be appreciated by those with that privilege, who may then graciously re-present the land to those who must be suffering its absence through living in the diaspora. Or, provide at least a taste of what they have missed to those who, by reason of poor birth, have missed out altogether.

This role is concurrent with his paid employment, since he is constantly on Skype, linking his office in Trinidad with suppliers in Europe or North America. Video-conference and webcamming have become a ubiquitous part of his work. He finds the visual aspect of webcam essential, if, for example, he is talking to an Italian who is not confident in standard English, let alone Trini-English. Their mutual fondness for gestures and bodily and facial expression makes this a much more effective mode of communication. His work also means that he has travelled a fair bit, and so his sense of Trinidad as special comes through this exposure to contrast. One of the most common constituents of this ambassadorial role, not just for Nikhil but for many Trinidadians, is Carnival. Trinidad is not a major tourist destination compared to other Caribbean islands, with few impressive beaches. The exception is Carnival, when the whole country seems to be on parade.

Nikhil gets a particular buzz from exploiting foreigners' surprise at more Indo-Trinidadian aspects of local culture. Nikhil is keen to correct the misapprehension that Trinidad is simply one more Caribbean population of exclusively African origin. Nikhil once took his webcam around with him on Divali to demonstrate to a US-based tourist how this has become an authentic Trini celebration. His Facebook pages are full of photos from Trinidad such as 'this is what my home looked like for Divali'.

At home, Nikhil's computer is in a public space, 'so it's not like it's my room or my mom's or dad's, so anyone could just, and the door is always open'. He loves travel and doesn't mind too much if he is actually visiting other countries, or seeing them through webcam. He loves to set up his relatives on Skype, thereby facilitating the expansion of their horizons. The important thing is that this should be visual. In the middle of a webcam conversation, he will hold up the toy or a fruit that he is discussing. 'Look what I got today, do you guys have this back at home?' He likes to see the expressiveness in other people, or have them play guitar online which he thinks would be boring without the visual component. He prefers face-to-face over always-on. His hobby is photography, another means to show his world to the world.

The reason for juxtaposing Jason and Nikhil is that they have equally seized upon the possibility of webcam for developing their relationship to location. As in our theory of attainment, they are seeing the potential of webcam in further developing visions that already existed, but had been technologically more difficult before. And yet, these visions represent two opposite extremes. Jason shows how webcam can be used to create authentic sociality derived from separating oneself from place as mere location, to produce a more analytically abstract and transcendent form of self in relation to others through art, while Nikhil uses webcam to reinforce the affective experience of visual immediacy through being able to see and therefore feel what it means to have a clear and grounded sense of location in the place where one is born.

A balancing act

The chapter started by claiming to go beyond the more established concern with webcam and location as arising from migration and diaspora. But having explored a range of other issues such as attention and domesticity, we return to this core issue. It would be quite a lacuna to ignore the impact of migration on an island such as Trinidad, where Miller (1994: 21) found that, even by the late 1980s, most Trinidadians were transnational at the nuclear level. Older Trinidadians today may find themselves living part of the year with a child in Canada, and other parts of that same year with a different child in London, and then with other relatives in Trinidad. This is a helpful reminder that, for many people, location is really kinship rather than place per se. This is something very evident from earlier anthropological studies. While there are some advantages to this transnational living – sensible Trinis will spend summers in the North and join the flock roosting in Trinidad for the winter – nevertheless, given the choice, these same Trinidadian parents would still have preferred to experience family simultaneously rather than sequentially. Webcam allows them to resolve these issues of distance and retain personal contact with all their kin. The next chapter focuses on the particular instance of webcam as part of grandparenting.

On occasion, it is the repair of a single relationship that counts, as with the person who communicated with her mother almost every day for eleven years but has little other transnational communication. More often, webcam is seen as coming to assist in a situation of such dispersed transnationalism, that there are no real alternatives to this virtual re-engagement. That is often how people introduce their relationship to webcam. A woman explained that her mother lives in Canada and a brother lives in the US. She also has both a sister and a brother in the UK. Of her friends, two are in the UK, one is in Chicago and two are in Canada. Another describes her friends as four in Canada, two in the UK, and five in the US but, of course, each in a different place within those countries.

Quite apart from migration and diaspora, there are an increasing number of Trinidadians who these days travel constantly as part of their work, often to several different countries. Or if their sister is living abroad, then it might be her who is sometimes in Russia and sometimes in China. This is a prime instance where it makes more sense to see the relationship as located on webcam itself, irrespective of physical location. Location mainly asserts itself as the inconvenience of incompatible time zones, which then reminds people of the materiality of spatial dispersion. Time constraints also mean that a busy mother online has a problem, as she speaks to her sister in Canada every day, but time differentials mean this has to happen at just the same time as she really needs to be with her children.

Webcam is used to reach a kind of existential *modus vivendi*, a balance between contact and absence that is intended to be sustainable in the long term. What people most want is literally 'the best of both worlds'. Gabriella, for example, says of her sister,

> in fact she says she doesn't need to come to Trinidad that often, she's seeing us, she's seeing the house, she's seeing what we are doing, how we are looking, so she say there's little need for her. The urgency, you know the craving to come back home, it's less, it's not as strong as it used to be. So it bridged a gap for her. So she likes to see things, she likes to see the rooms and all of that, so she gets to see it. Like if we paint the wall she wants to see the colour, if we put up the Christmas tree she wants to see the colour. She plant some plants before she left, like when she was on vacation, she wants to see if they're growing so they take it outside, all of that, anything, she wants to see it. *[How often do you show*

> *her things?]* Well, she does want to see, but I don't like that too much, so I will tell her some other time, right, I always put her off. But all in all, I'd say once in two weeks I'd show her something, but she wouldn't mind if you show her around every day, but it would mean I'd have to walk around, yeah so maybe once in two weeks.

Gabriella imagines that under this new webcam regime, her sister would be comfortable returning to Trinidad about once every two years.

Similarly, a Brazilian recalls how he became reconciled to being abroad:

> I did miss home around Christmas but, it's a comparative thing. So when I first got to London and I was there and my family was all here, I was studying, I was doing my masters and stuff I would have missed home a great deal more then. Then I was able to interact with them via MSN which was years later. So comparative when I got to London, say the first 5 years compared to the last 5 years it was very different, technology helped in a big way. I can't imagine just how much I spent in phone bills the first few years I lived in London.

As webcam simultaneously adds visual contact and subtracts the expense, the general assumption is that it is much easier to be away from one's country of birth than used to be the case. A common sentiment is that 'They miss it less, they feel more at home, they miss it less, right, because they interact with all who home, so they really feel like they are home.'

Eventually, if someone is away long enough and things are working out, this may shift from a balance of partial autonomy to the loss of the relationship as in: 'I don't think she misses Trinidad to that extent, that connection to Trinidad is slowly being lost, but I think she wants her presence in Trinidad because of her family.' A highly significant extension of webcam for Trinidadians has become the transnational viewing of a funeral. In the past, even if people were quite removed from family life in Trinidad, there was a strong expectation that they should be present for a funeral and the associated wake. If webcam is accepted as a substitute for family occasions, this will make a real impact on the number of return visits, for example:

> I'll tell you, my cousin, his mom passed away and her son, who was living in Miami for a long time, who never couldn't make any arrangements to get his papers, couldn't come to the funeral, and couldn't come to anything cos it was difficult to him. So when we had the service, he was there by webcam. And when we had the prayer meeting, he was there by webcam, that was part of it. And my parents had their 50th anniversary, or 51st or whatever, but it was a significant anniversary and my sister wasn't here, but she was there by webcam.

So, in returning to the initial issue of whether webcam repairs the breach in family life created by migration, we find that this is often the case. But that is only part of the story as, equally often, this blends into our wider point about trying to re-think webcam more as a place people live in rather than just connecting two other places. We need to start thinking of a new kind of transnationalism, which incorporates the life online as an integral part of location itself. We conclude by reinforcing this point through an extended example which reveals the whole gamut of ways people today can feel part of life in all three locations, in this case London, Trinidad and also online. Monique manages to sustain all three and also the relationships between them.

Monique and Transnational Domestic Life

One of the advantages of the example of Monique, who has already been introduced in Chapter Three, is that she helps to distance us from seeing these problems merely in terms of technology and affordances. Monique detests technology and remains quite disdainful of any interest in media per se. Webcam for her is a relationship, analogous with those she cultivates with people, home, pets and possessions. The relationship she most literally cultivates is gardening. Texts on Caribbean anthropology and history have tended to be firmly focused on 'the yaard', the area around the house where people have tended to plant flowers and foods for immediate consumption (Abrahams, 1983). These were important in the recapturing of family and domestic life after slavery.

Monique would not let a little thing like being in London get in the way of cultivating her yard. After a thorough inspection via webcam, she will tell her mother when her sweet potato plant needs to have its roots softened or when to dig it up. She needs about three inspections a month to retain her control over what's going on. It's important because it's something of a battleground out there: 'We have one long sweet potato vine that is taking over a whole stretch, and it's battling with a pumpkin vine that came up out of nowhere, and then a pawpaw tree just appeared in the midst of everything and we're like "where did you come from?" But it's there and it's growing and we get nice pawpaw from it.'

The other prosthetic is her husband: 'I was like "well it's time for you to transplant, because it's like one mammee aloes and like fifteen baby aloes. I mean come on" and he's like "alright, alright" so I think he's gonna transplant it the week after next week. And I bought all the materials when I was there. So I have to tell him in which order everything goes and literally talk him through the process via Skype. Yeah I watch what he's doing.' This then extends to her relationship with her mother-in-law: 'So she'll tell me she had to beg my husband to do this and I'll be like "Oh, he's letting my plant die" and we'll chat and she'll chat about her family because she's a proper country girl, she grew up in . . . So we'll talk about fruits, what fruits are in season, yeah.' For Monique, the lack of sociability in London is closely linked to the lack of anywhere to plant anything. Everything just seems to be concrete, and in her student accommodation she is reduced to a pot of basil. Without this vicarious gardening through webcam she thinks she would go crazy.

Despite the evident efficiencies, Monique insists that her media of choice is letter writing. It's so frustrating that when she writes such letters, often on handmade paper, she expects some acknowledgement of the care and concern she feels she has expressed. Instead, she gets complaints that her letters are just so long. With an affinity for history and literature – which she has taught at secondary school – she sees this as something important to her sense of herself, and she still sends around six letters and ten postcards a month. Monique is the kind of person who would only have accepted webcam on the grounds that some relationships needed this. It was originally her students at the secondary school in Trinidad who pushed for using webcam so they could show her things directly, both writing and images. For once, she felt that the technologies were not trying to distance her, but were meeting her half way, even though she still felt there were serious limitations. With mere webcam, there could be no 'Hey let's go out and get something to eat', but at least webcam was a kind of face-to-face.

Still, she doesn't trust webcam any more than any other aspect of the internet. She describes herself as paranoid, and her real technical expertise is in the field of firewalls and virus protection. She is very careful about what she shares, certainly no incriminating pictures. She was furious when she found a tagged picture of herself in a university publication that she had not authorized. She is fairly ambivalent about Facebook, recognizing the paradox that she, like many others, mainly spread anti-Facebook propaganda – on Facebook. She adds friends and then deletes them again, causing a certain amount of concern. The problem is that she doesn't feel that a thing like Facebook can have evolved a proper etiquette, which is what social intercourse should be based on.

Curiously, the event that completely converted her and entirely humanized webcam as far as she was concerned was not even human; it was her cat. Since Monique was thirteen, she and her cat would stare at each other and the cat would listen to her voice. Early on, the cat would also stare for long periods at the webcam. For whatever reason, Monique's cat didn't seem able to have babies (Monique uses the word *babies*, never 'a litter'). And then when she was quite old she had some, but Monique was already living in London. Then one day, the cat took each of her babies, picked them up by their necks and deposited them one by one in front of the webcam. Not even Monique thinks the cat understands the webcam as a visual medium, but this seems to her (and even to us) indisputable evidence that the cat understands the implications of the computer as a source of Monique's voice. In any case, her family had often brought the cat to the webcam, since Monique was so concerned to see her while she has been away. Monique's mother's dog also seems to get excited when he hears her voice; he jumps up and down and on one occasion managed to topple the laptop from the desk to the floor, though it survived.

It's a common thing in Trinidad for parents to worry that their children are *magga* – too thin, and Monique admits that magga was pretty much her nickname when she was young and stayed around 90 pounds. The mere fact that she is living in London is no barrier to the level of detail her mother, a nurse, will go into to check on her health. Webcam is often an 'in your face' medium, but with Monique, it's going right inside her mouth with her tongue sticking out so her mother can inspect her teeth, which are also considered too small to be healthy, plus Monique is known to be too fond of sweets. If she sees dry skin on Monique's face, then she also wants to see her arms and elbows. This is a clear indication that the water in London must be bad or have some kind of deposit in it. Both of them are into natural remedies, but while she can get aloe vera, which is her mother's solution to most ailments, other bush medicines would have to be sent from Trinidad. It's not just health; the close webcam reveals how many split ends Monique has and how damaged her hair is. But webcams don't have to be static, so her mother can also check that her daughter is keeping up her standards. She insists the drawers are opened to see that clothes have been folded up and not just stuffed inside, as Monique sometimes did even when in Trinidad. Once, she even insisted on seeing her sneakers to see if they were dusty. Monique has five identical and supremely comfortable pairs that cost next to nothing in Trinidad, which she calls her '*alloo* pies' because they have the shape of the East Indian potato pie. Once the room and clothes have been inspected, then finally Monique has to angle the webcam so her mother can check that she has unplugged any other devices and most of all locked the doors 'because you know these people in those foreign countries – they're psychopaths'.

For Monique's mother, both health and behaviour reflect on something equally important, which is spiritual well-being. Monique's mother comes from what in Trinidad is called a 'shouter Baptist' tradition, which stems from the more syncretic union of Christianity with West African, mainly Yoruba, religion. Monique herself has dabbled with Pentecostalism, with being a Jehovah's Witness at least in their opposition to what she sees as the fake festival of Christmas. She even had a flirtation with Islam, though never as fully as her brother, whose identification with Islam is now well entrenched.

Fortunately, these webcam inspections can only take place at weekends. Her mother is even more technophobic than Monique. They depend on Monique's husband, Adam, who has also remained in Trinidad and brings around the laptop for his in-laws to use. But once it is set up for her, Monique's mother doesn't really regard the laptop as technology. Often, Adam goes over at two o'clock and is still there at seven o'clock:

> Yeah it's a long process, because by the time I chat with my dad and my granddad is living there and he has to cry, every time he sees me he has to cry and he makes me cry to. So by the time I go through my granddad and my dad that's like two and a half hours. And sometimes my brothers are there and they have to tell me a whole set of stories and how work was and what they did and by the time I get to my mom it's probably later down in the evening and we chat and whatever and she examines me and sometimes I tell my husband I want to see the yard today so that that's the first thing that gets done because if I don't I wouldn't see the yard. So yeah it could be five hours or more.

In the end, Monique had to teach her mother to use webcam and set her up with a laptop during one of her return visits. The reason had nothing to do with keeping in touch; it was because her mother got vexed with the phone company, at which point she just threw out the landline. She would only use the internet when Monique had promised her this was provided by the cable company Flow, and had nothing to do with the phone company. Her mother was then astonished to find she could have her phone back again through the cable company: 'Really, they have phone?' Still, her mother will keep asking, 'Can you see me, can you see me?' Fortunately, there is a rather more comfortable webcam relationship she can have, which is with her sister who lives separately and where neither are bothered too much whether the webcam itself is on or off, as long as they are still chatting through Skype.

The visual aspect of webcam does matter, however, in that they tend to talk quite a bit about their problems with hair: 'Well both of us have natural hair so we'd swap recipes for stuff, because we don't buy anything because we can't find anything that works on our hair the way we want it to, so I'll be like "yeah I used this this week and the hair was pretty soft and I comb it this week" and she'll be like "really, I'll try it," actually I happened to talk to her this week and I showed her because I flat ironed my hair so I could cut it.' In some ways, Monique's sister is rather more excited than Monique about her being in London, seeing that there are all those cheap clothes that Monique can buy at Primark. So, Monique is planning to send back a barrel. Barrels are a well-established Caribbean tradition for sending back goods from the diaspora. Jamaican children, whose parents had migrated to the UK, were called 'barrel children' for the goods parents sent them in lieu of their presence.

Webcam, then, takes its place in a whole gamut of relationships with various family members, but also her relationship to her pets, the yard and the home. There is also the relationship between webcam and other media. For her father, the letters are too slow, so webcam provides the basis of everyday interaction. Yet, the letters still give him something tangible that webcam cannot. It's not just that she shows him her meals so that he can be reassured that she is eating properly; she shows him each stage of cooking, from boiling the rice, to which kind of sugar she is using. While with a friend, there is a constant flow between SMS and webcamming that works more with the informality of friendship itself.

What is noteworthy also about Monique is that this attention to the much wider sphere of the yard, the pets and her extended family does not detract at all from the other central role of webcam in maintaining her primary relationship to her husband. They have been married four years, and always knew that marrying after her degree could well mean subsequent separation for a post-graduate degree. Indeed, this may have precipitated marriage as a demonstration of their mutual commitment. At the same time, the prospect of webcam meant that separation didn't sound quite so bad, along with the ability to be together during vacations. The way webcam conveys the intimacy in their relationship was described in Chapter Three.

Pre-empting our discussion of polymedia in Chapter Six, it seems that far from signalling the end of more material communication such as writing, this couple use webcam to finesse more traditional media. 'Yeah, because if I'm writing something and I'm not sure, I'd be like "how does this sound?" or I'll load up the file and he'll check it. So during writing periods, the Skype is really nice because I'll be like "should I use 'are' here? Should I use were or was?" because he's actually pretty alright at grammar, and I'm not.' Alternatively, they might talk about politics or what was in the Trinidad newspapers. Skype had become their daily routine, chatting for a while, then leaving it on until it tended to just drop. A couple of times a month, they would turn to the phone for much more extended conversations. The visual aspect of Skype returns Monique to her role in the home.

Not only does she look at their cats and dogs, but she frequently asks to look at the car. In Trinidad, the car is often something more like a living room and used to be the subject of constantly changing interiors. Her husband has this toy monkey that he leaves on the front of his dashboard, and sometimes he'll put a jacket or shoes or shades or a chain on it and he'd put him in different poses:

> So I'll like to see what it is he did with the monkey, what's the new development with the monkey. And well I have stuffed toys there and I'll tell him – well they need a dusting, and I'll tell him which one I want to move to the front, and which one to put where, because I want them all to have their chance in the front, yeah, this is all done through webcam. And sometimes I would want something changed in the room, or I'd remember that I have a product that's expiring, and I'll tell him – throw it out . . . And I'll tell him how to do it and you know where I put stuff, because I kinda organize our banking information. So I have like a file for that, so when I now came I had to tell him, well I labelled it and everything. So when you get these statements, put them here, and your pay slips here, and I walked him through his tax returns.

Conclusion

One of the principal aims of our theory of attainment is simply to reconfirm various quite conventional anthropological perspectives. We feel that the hype of technology studies and the more judgemental cultural studies have deflected us from the more sober and patient commitment to analyse behaviour as the comparative study of cultural normativity. Our theory argues that the focus should move from seeing new technology as changing what it means to be human, and instead see it as just another set of examples of cultural diversity that shed light on the myriad ways there are to be human. So the intention of this chapter, as with the previous two substantive chapters, is to indicate how peering through the lens of webcam is a bit like some kind of x-ray that reveals the internal structures of ideology masked by the flabby exterior of unreflective and uncritical acceptance; our Copernican revolution that sees media as a place we live in and helps throw into the foreground all those presumptions about domesticity or the elision of attention and presence that had become simply normative.

Whether we examine children trying to escape from the confines of their bedroom, or Monique refusing to even acknowledge what others see as the limits of webcam, we are made alert to the way people cultivate webcam to grow all sorts of new ways of configuring social life. Yet, the most radical discovery may be how change facilitates convention. Somehow, hearing about someone in London still bothering to follow their family household division of labour, right down to the task of checking the plants, filling in the tax returns and cleaning the car interior, provides a sense of completeness to this picture of transnational domestic life, such that we forget how fantastic this would have been before the advent of webcam.

But, then, it wasn't just Monique who has pushed the possibilities of webcamming; it was also her cat, and this may be the final piece in our jigsaw, since Monique was not alone in this. It is curious how often people talked about the importance of seeing a cat or dog through webcam; how significant, and especially how exciting this was, the moment they could squeal with pleasure. Certainly, we do not want to detract from people's genuine affection for their pets, but there seemed more to this. It was noticeable how the pets often in turn were reflections upon a relationship: a couple not yet ready to have children, but sharing the pet that seemed to speak to the maturity of their relationship, or in another case, the puppy the boyfriend had bought as a present. As well as relationships in their own right, pets serve well as vicarious signs of other relationships, where they make it easier to express unqualified enthusiasm. These are also household pets, and may therefore also correspond to a commitment to place. One of the themes of this chapter has been the de-stabilizing impact of webcam that reveals the pervious quality to bricks and mortar. It is not the material substance of place, but our relationship to place that is crucial here. We have found that this is most effectively accomplished when it remains subservient to the wider set of relationships. When Monique's cat brought her kittens to the webcam, it was as though the house itself was reminding her of their mutual commitments, and that Monique and her home, in its cat aspect, really do care about each other. This is Monique's sense of place.

5

Maintaining Relationships

The heart of this volume must be a chapter on relationships. While our participants might be interested in some of the previous discussions around self-consciousness or location or intimacy, these might still seem to them somewhat peripheral to the main purpose they generally ascribe to their use of Skype and other webcam platforms. Their primary concern is simply the maintenance of relationships. Technology is a means but relationships are the ends. The ability to maintain a relationship is usually held to be the primary reason why people are happy or sad in life. While these include a variety of friendships, the most common primary relationships are those of kinship, at least if one includes the couple as incipient kinship. This would be particularly true of our Trinidadian material. Our core informants, often of East Indian origin and living in a small town, have lives dominated by relationships constituted by kinship.

Anthropological study began with research dedicated to such worlds dominated by and organized by kinship. The great names of British social anthropology, Malinowski, Radcliffe-Brown, Evans-Pritchard and Fortes sought to understand how small-scale societies maintained order and structure without the organization of states and governments (Carsten, 2003, Godelier, 2012). In *After Kinship*, Carsten (2003: 10) describes how they saw kinship as political structure, providing the basis for social order and function. Recently, Godelier (2012) has revisited both the general scholarship on kinship and his own extensive experience in the study of the Baruya within tribal New Guinea. He charts the continuities of practices and rituals and the transformation of meanings from a society that governed itself and its own territory largely through the norms of kinship to the creation of modern citizenship through the intervention of the state.

Since the 1970s, kinship studies have tended to focus less on order and structure and more on everyday experiences and the contradictions, paradoxes and ambivalence within nuclear, extended and separated families, transnational families and discussions around new reproductive technologies (Peletz, 1995; Godelier, 2012). This culminated in the work of Carsten (2007, 2003). For the early anthropological studies, kinship was a given order of the world, which largely determined behaviour, as people were expected to act as, for example, a mother's brother should to a sister's son. But in Carsten's work, we reach the opposite end of a spectrum of analysis in which there is the possibility that it is behaviour that in part makes kinship, so that the person who acts as a father is constituted as a father.

Miller (2008b) takes issue with Carsten, arguing that even in contemporary Britain, with high divorce rates and subsequently complex relationships, people's behaviour remains circumscribed by the normative expectations of key kinship roles. He focuses more on the tension between the expectations and experience, the discrepancy between how an ideal mother should act and one's actual mother. But for a discipline such as anthropology, this type of analytical discussion must always remain subservient to ethnographic evidence and, not surprisingly, we find that some societies seem closer to Carsten's arguments and others less. Indeed, Miller's first (1994) ethnographic writing about kinship in Trinidad looks much closer to Carsten than to his own arguments, in that there is far more emphasis on kinship as voluntaristic than would be the case in Britain. In Caribbean families, the woman who gave birth to a child was not necessarily the same woman who reared a child; people and their roles within families could be swapped around (Ho, 1993; Clarke, 1999; Chamberlain, 2003). One cousin may be merely a cousin, while another becomes a best friend, again allowing an element of choice to intrude within the structure of kinship.

If we start to think of kinship as partly constituted by behaviour, then we can also imagine technology as helping to constitute a relationship through its impacts upon behaviour. A frequently noted result of new digital technologies is that they disrupt our prior ideas as to the proper relationship between the generations. One woman in El Mirador told us about her daughter and her mother. Her daughter at three years old had her own iPod Touch with which she would webcam her grandmother every day at whatever time she chose. She could easily turn it on, swipe, select the icon and find the contact (through the photo). In addition, she would help her mother when the latter couldn't find things on her own phone. Meanwhile, that same grandmother in New York had just found a new partner. But when confronted, she confessed to her daughter that she had met him online, at which point her daughter had given her mother the usual lecture on having failed to take precautions before meeting people they only knew from online. In effect, she was mothering her mother and being mothered by her daughter.

To understand the place of this technology as attainment, or when repairing the breach of a separated relationship, something that could equally be called retainment, we need to keep these various perspectives in balance. On the one hand, as Miller argues, we have to acknowledge the strong constraints that remain based on traditional ideas of kinship as structure. However, as prior studies of the family in Trinidad have shown, there are considerable variations in family structure, which are only partly explained by the diverse ethnic origins of the population (Klass, 1961; Rodman, 1971). This means that with kinship, we are examining a phenomenon that contains strong elements of cultural specificity. For this reason, this chapter differs from the others in that all the examples come from our Trinidad fieldwork. It would be too confusing if we strayed beyond this regional focus. At the same time, we accept that there is also a tremendous amount of creative and emotional energy that is given to lived relationships (Carsten, 2003). Following Miller (2008b), our means of keeping these points in balance is through examining the way any given kinship role includes the idealized model of that kin category – what mothers and children are respectively supposed to be like. Then there is the actual person who inhabits the category of mother or child, and finally there is the discrepancy that inevitably exists between these two.

These points can apply to each particular kinship role. Given the constraints of space, this chapter will confine itself to a couple of examples. Yet, there is also another relationship which is discussed just as much in Trinidad; the relationship to that collective noun – *the family*:

> Who was living there was my grandma's sister, her daughter, and then her daughter had two kids, and then her daughter had a friend . . . no, it was a sister who had another kid who was living with them but the sister wasn't living with them, and then someone's cousin was living there too. *[So basically you webcammed them?]* All of them, it was never just one of them, if they were all home, they were all on the webcam. They would huddle around the computer when someone else is on. It's like you are the TV programme they are watching. So the family will come and sit together and it was the main event.

Parents

One of the factors that complicates our analysis is that the ideals of any given kinship role now derive from forces other than simply tradition or custom. This is because, from at least the 1950s onwards, psychology and other academic studies have themselves become a primary source of ideology and normative expectation around kinship, for example with respect to expected norms of caring and nurturing (Smart and Neale, 1999; Carsten, 2003). Specifically, newspapers and other popular media continue to promulgate ideas about what a good mother should be, based on vulgarized versions of psychoanalysts such as Bowlby (1988) and Winnicott (1960). As a result, the ideal of a close, unmediated reliance of the child upon the mother has almost become a universal principle and moral judgement upon each generation of parents.

For example, Sherelle, a mother in her early fifties, has five children, four of whom are working while one is still in high school. Thinking about the role her youngest son's iPhone is playing in his life she states: 'I feel sorry for these children, the times is so different, yuh can't go out all hours of the night walk back, yuh jus go to school an come home, go to school an come home. So they jus textin all the time and chatting, they don't get to spend time together anymore, there's so much less meaningful interaction.' We often hear similar sentiments that seem to express what the newspapers and TV now regard as the proper parent's lament. New media become seen as an unholy mediation that supplants the 'natural' or 'proper' relationship. But taken from Sherelle as our informant we would fully acknowledge this as her authentic voice. In their study of Filipina mothers working in London, both Trinidadian traditions and these new international norms have strongly gendered concepts of parenting. Mothering is associated with feeding, nurturing and care-giving (Durkheim, 1997; Parsons and Bales, 1956; Barlow and Chapin, 2010). Fathers, on the other hand, are often seen as more 'instrumental' in fostering social competence in children by way of being punitive, restrictive and playing more of a disciplinarian role. Fathers transmit educative functions and skills, whose degree of transmission reflects their degree of involvement (Hewlett, 1991). The efficacy of webcam then becomes a judgement on its ability to transmit these expected roles of mothering/fathering, overcoming the spatial and temporal constraints of separation. In this section, we provide two examples, one that focuses more on issues of fatherhood and the other upon mothering.

Previously, Caribbean parenting, with its history of often absent baby-fathers (see Clarke, 1999; Chevannes, 2001; Miller and Maiter, 2008) and strict mothering, were very different from those of the UK, for example. Today, in Trinidad, even with the influence of global norms fostered by psychologists, the legacy of these differences remains. Fatherhood can be a good deal more fragile from the start, since disputing paternity is something of a national pastime. For example, on LexoTV, a Trinidadian YouTube phenomenon based loosely on Sesame Street-style puppets, a priest warns a recalcitrant child, 'I will go and tell yuh mother and yuh fathers.' Both traditional and more recent norms maintain distinctions between mothering and fathering roles. Typically, we found in Trinidad that children have stronger relationships with their mothers, discussing a wider variety of topics, especially more social and personal issues (Socha and Stamp, 1995; Barlow and Chapin, 2010), but would expect to consult with fathers about plans for the future and attitudes towards public and political issues (Noller and Fitzpatrick, 1993), academic achievement and instrumental tasks.

Emily

In analysing our evidence, we are never really talking just about the impact of webcam; it is inevitably webcam as a concomitant effect of the simultaneous experience of separation. Either and both of these may exacerbate or resolve the tensions inherent in such parenting roles. Emily, for example, talked to her parents together over webcam while she was working as a volunteer in Haiti in her early twenties. She would describe her day, the differences she found in the culture and the difficulties and frustrations of doing volunteer work. Her mother would be the more active discussant, asking questions and counselling her; meanwhile, her father would just listen, sometimes sitting at the computer with her mother, at other times, sitting on his armchair watching the television on mute. For Emily's father, not looking at Emily on the screen, just hearing her voice as though she was talking to her mother in the room, was more reminiscent of how things used to be when she was at home. Mainly, he wouldn't ask if she was well, or if she'd eaten and if she was taking care of herself, because these questions would force him to confront the distance created by her living abroad, and acknowledging that the stakes were much higher than when they were living together.

It was clear that Emily's father actually worried a great deal about such issues, but he had always been more of the silent support. As a result, Emily's mother would often have to deal with her husband's anxiety once the Skype call had ended, when he would express all his fears. On Skype, however, they presented the same kind of complementary forms of care and attention that helped to reassure Emily that things had not really changed. They would listen rather than think of burdening Emily with their own problems.

The point is that these respective roles of mother and father were experienced as complementary and effective when Emily was at home, where a mother could be more emotional and immediate and a father more considered and detached. But the use of webcam betokened a much greater separation, which then exacerbates the distance a 'proper' father feels from his daughter. At this point, the father feels disconnected and frustrated. They have chosen to maintain the form and style of this relationship but this had failed to maintain the affective relationship that the father desired with respect to his daughter. As we suggested, webcam impacts upon behaviour and thereby our ability to constitute relationships, although, in this case, the example is negative, as the father has become increasingly anxious because he feels the father's role has disappeared from the new webcam-based configuration. Such negative instances are just as helpful as positive ones in extending our understanding of prevalent gender roles in parenting, here adding to our appreciation of the fragility of the father's role.

Our informants also claimed that such experiences gave them insights into the nature of parenting. When she returned from abroad, Emily lived at home with her parents for a few months before moving out again. She remembers that time as being an especially good period for her and her parents. The communicative relationship they had created on Skype eased her re-entry into her role of adult child at home. 'Daddy asked was there anything I particularly missed while I was away, then he would say, "come on then, let's go to the mall, I'll treat you to lunch," and I could see he was quite happy to share the company and eat without necessarily having a conversation. Mummy on the other hand was happy to sit there and work things out whatever was going on with you.' The combination of separation and webcam provided the foundation for an acceptable degree of autonomy and appreciation of parental love and care that helped in the maturation of this parent–daughter relationship.

Nadine and Alia

Nadine, whose parents divorced in the early 1960s, when her mother migrated, leaving her to be brought up by her father's sister's family, is extremely mindful of how she acts as a mother to her two daughters. Now, in her early forties and practising as a relationship therapist in Port of Spain, Nadine is still coming to terms with her own relationship to her parents. Her focus is on sharing household tasks with her husband while concentrating on being the steady emotional rock for her daughters. She has a close but different relationship with each. Her oldest daughter Alia, at 20, has been studying for 18 months in Barbados. They treat her home visits as though these were designated holidays. Nadine feels she has a close and open relationship with Alia, whom she believes has the same warm and bubbly personality as herself.

While in Barbados, Alia would spend nearly three hours every couple of days on Skype with her mother: 'I relate better with Mommy, we talk about everything under the sun, so we have a different connection and she can understand a lot about my life and I can understand a lot about her life, so that's why we talk so much.' The entire family is active in their religious practices, and Alia and Nadine have also created a bond based on shared beliefs and ideas surrounding divinity and spirituality.

For Alia, who is very dedicated to her studies, the visual contact with her mother contributes to an emotional intensity.

> Depending on the situation and because of the relationship that we have, when I look at her, I feel emotional. For whatever reason. So if I do have something happy to say then I would look at her directly, actually I had an experience like that. I got an A in one of my courses, and the first person I wanted to talk to was mum, so I called her and as soon as I saw her I just wanted to cry, I couldn't even tell her what was going on. And it was difficult to look at her then, but I was glad that she was able to see me and I could see her when I was able to look at her. Just to know that of course, she's there. I called her I said hi, she was excited of course, she said hi, I told her that the results came out, and that's when I started to break down and of course she kept looking at me and she said I'm sure it can't be that bad and that's when I broke down even more, and I tried to tell her about it and I was crying so much my voice was broken I had to repeat it like 3 or 4 times to get a clear message across and I said 'Mom I got an A' and she started to cry too! I actually maximize the screen, I always maximize the screen whenever I talk to her. So I can feel like she's right there in front of me in life size figure. At that time, she just told me to go ahead and cry, so that's what I did, I cried for a few minutes and when I recovered, we talked normally.

Even when Alia told us this story, one could see the tears welling up again. She will speak with her father about life in Barbados and her studies, but not with the same detail.

It helps that Nadine uses Skype for her work and is therefore logged on for most of the day. When Alia is online, Nadine feels her daughter knows that she is there if she needs to talk to her. 'I would be at my desk and she would say "Mom, are you busy?" and I would say "never for you" and I would drop everything at work and just zone into her because I know she wouldn't call out to me unless something was really disturbing her and I could give her that emotional support because that's what she needed.'

For Nadine, being able to see Alia compensates for not being able to hug her or touch her, as she is a very tactile person, touching your arm or your hand, while speaking with you.

> Sometimes I will touch the screen or say I'm touching your face now, and I'm touching your hand, or we touch the screen together or blow kisses. It brings a certain amount of peace, but this is after we have really communicated or brought our feelings back out in the open, at the end of the conversation. I would never start a conversation with her like, to me the emotions are too heightened at that time for me to even go into there, because if I were to do that, I would allow all my emotions to run and then I wouldn't be able to be that support that I know I should be. This child has always had such a big energy for me. Sometimes when she was smaller and I was tired or feeling drained and she would want to climb on me and hug me, I just couldn't because it was too overwhelming. I think I do that to her too.

The key difference between using webcam and speaking face-to-face with Alia is that Nadine has to make a lot more effort to keep a hold on her emotions when using webcam.

We presented these two particular cases since they stand for the wider generalizations from our Trinidad fieldwork, though ones with many exceptions. It seemed to us that fatherhood starts from a more fragile position. As a result, this combination of separation and webcam may exacerbate tensions and the feeling of distance, but then, as in the case of Emily's father, these may also be resolved, if, as here, they come into alignment with the growing autonomy of older children. By contrast, in the case of motherhood, the centrality of intense and emotional engagement that was considered the norm prior to separation fits well with the intensity of webcam's in-your-face experience, such that Nadine and Alia find it still more emotional and harder to control than in the already highly charged atmosphere of the mother–daughter relationship.

Grandparents and toddlers

One of the key concerns amongst the elderly, suggested by research in many regions, is the need to combat feelings of loneliness (van der Geest, 2002; Yeh and Sing, 2004; Rawlins et al., 2008). Elderly people who experience physical difficulties and disabilities that affect their mobility find it more difficult to keep up with their social contacts and yet, at the same time, there is an increasing dependency on others for daily support (Yeh and Sing, 2004). Older adults who are more active in keeping autonomy and independence and who are still working, either full- or part-time, claim to have a higher quality of life, based on relationships with families, friends, neighbours and having a secure home and livelihood (Alavi et al., 2011).

Vera

Vera is in her late seventies and lives with her husband in their family home. All of her children have families of their own; some live nearby and her day-to-day activities revolve around what needs to be done on their behalf, rather than being entertained, or relaxing. 'Keeping busy' is her main way to spend the day, most of which is cooking and housework. Such days start at 6 a.m. and she works through till midday. She takes care of her husband, who is not as mobile now he has had hip replacement surgery. He wakes, watches the morning news and waits for his breakfast at eight o'clock. From eleven, Vera rests and logs onto Skype and Facebook for the first of three sessions in the day. Her sons in England and Canada are not yet online, given the time difference, so she doesn't expect to speak with anyone, but she likes to see what posts or photos have been updated by her grandchildren overnight.

She may click on an update or go straight to the page of a grandchild and see what has caught their interest over the week. Vera is less interested in their sharing of humorous photos, memes or music video clips. She will focus on photos they've put up of where they are, who they're with and what they are doing. If there is a new album of a wedding or holiday or night out, so much the better. Then she will go though each photo, 'liking' them, or leaving comments. Later in the morning, her son Chris usually signs onto Skype from Canada. Chris works afternoon shifts and his wife has just had a baby. She has continued her night shifts a few days a week, allowing her and Chris to tag-team. So she will sleep in the day and take care of their young son in the evening before Chris returns from work. Chris and Vera usually Skype every second day or so, for hours at a time. Sometimes Chris continues to do things on the computer and Vera watches him and her grandson sitting on his lap. Other times, Chris carries on with what he is doing in the background and the detachable webcam is placed where Vera can see the baby playing on the floor or sitting in his high chair at a table.

For Vera, her regular visual contact with Chris offers two things; firstly, she and her grandson would not know each other if it wasn't for the constant visual communication. Chris and his family have not yet had the opportunity to come to Trinidad since the baby was born. Secondly, Vera's life is largely homebound. She is only able to leave home when one of her sons or daughters takes her into town or on a visit to a relative. Mostly she stays at home to care for her husband. Skype has given her the chance to have company while she is at home, otherwise she would be 'staring at the four walls'. Since marrying at a young age, Vera has largely been defined by her role as a homemaker and caregiver. Although she has a large family and several grandchildren, even these are mainly grown up, with only one young grandchild in Trinidad. The others tend to visit her with their families on weekends, but seldom during the week when they are busy.

Webcam has become one of the most important parts of Vera's daily routine and a major source of company. She keeps her laptop on the bed; she logs on in mid-morning and then will move it to the gallery until mid-afternoon. She checks it sporadically to see who's online and if someone is available to talk, she calls them. Going to bed in the evening provides Vera with her final intensive time online. This works well both because late at night is her down time, and also the time when more of her friends and relatives living abroad are online. This is when she and Chris have their longer face-to-face talks. He has told Vera several times that although he likes living in Toronto (where he has now been for several years), he still finds it difficult not having family support just down the road. It's something he has never gotten used to. So Vera feels this is her opportunity to provide him with emotional support as his mother as well as share his company.

Some of this evidence overlaps with the previous section on parenting. But in addition, there is an important symmetrical relationship between the oldest and the youngest members of the household. Webcam works particularly well at both ends of the spectrum, partly because it is experienced less as a technology and more as a sense of immediacy with another person. This is especially true of the toddlers, who, depending on their age, might not be able to recognize and relate to a person through a phone call but can respond at first in limited ways but later with enthusiastic recognition to webcam, while elderly people can appropriate webcam as something more like a television screen than a new technology.

Noller and Fitzpatrick (1993) note that babies under six months old are able to differentiate human faces, they try to communicate with them, respond when they are spoken to and respond to positive involvement, as part of the developmental stage of recognizing their capacity for being worthwhile and identifying trustworthiness in other people. Observations of babies over webcam show early interactive skills of smiling, vocalization and gazing, which is consistent with face-to-face communication (Socha and Stamp, 1995). Chris's eight-month-old son would respond to his grandmother's voice and face initially in their video calls, by smiling and staring at her image, but would lose attention quickly. When we were present in the call, we could not hold his attention or recognition, presumably because we were much less familiar to him than Vera. Similarly, Shandelle, who uses Skype predominantly so her husband can see their four-month-old son, described how he was extremely responsive when he heard his father's voice. 'Every time the baby sees the computer, he thinks Daddy is there because that's how he interacts with him. He knows once the computer comes up, he is looking and it's the same with a phone, he expects to hear his daddy's voice. But the minute you turn Skype on and you put the video call on, he starts babbling to him.'

Sherlon, who mostly uses Skype with his brother in the UK as always-on, first introduced his 12-month-old son to his 10-month-old cousin in the UK over Skype and saw how the children responded to each other. He describes how he knew there was another baby looking at him: 'He was just amazed, he was like "he's there!" and he pointed at him. He would be touching the screen and he would hear words from his uncle in the background and he would react.' Sherlon's wife often webcammed him at work when their son was misbehaving and he would assume the fatherly role of disciplinarian over webcam. 'And if he's giving trouble, she will call me and say watch what your son is doing and he will see me and start to laugh and stop giving trouble a bit, but when it goes off, back to trouble again.'

Toddlers may also use webcam as simple face-to-face communication. Shania uses webcam with her 18-month-old daughter when speaking with her sister in the US. The aunt and niece have never met in person, but have seen each other over Skype since the niece was a baby:

> She'll speak to her, she knows that her aunty hears her and she knows that she can see her also, so sometimes she will wave at them, so that they will wave back and she'll say certain things, so she knows, she understands they're there. She probably doesn't understand how, why the gap is between. But that's how she developed her own little relationship with her aunty, whom she has never seen before. She would come up and, well she doesn't say much words yet, she's still learning, but she will babble with her, and my sister will understand and talk back. Sometimes I will leave them sitting there, Jenny sitting at the computer and my sister, and I'm off making a bottle or whatever and come back and they're still chatting. So she has developed that relationship with her aunt because of how frequent she interacts with her online, and sometimes I am not even there and they're chatting away, both of them.

There is a clear symmetry between the elderly, on the one hand, and the very young, on the other, based essentially on their respective dependency: the child who can only recognize the grandparent with the visual cues of webcam, and the grandparent who is equally incapacitated by reasons of decreasing mobility. One of the pleasures of such research is witnessing the subsequent delight older people feel in this new capacity to both see and interact with their grandchildren or even great-grandchildren even when they now live in another country.

Siblings

Sibling relationships are usually the longest relationships experienced over a lifetime, founded in the intimate daily contact of shared childhood, and often retained as adults (Cicirelli, 1995). We should therefore anticipate that this would be a relationship that would take readily to webcam especially when separated, for example by living in separate countries. More generalized studies suggest that while gender may be a factor, generally siblings relate to each other as equals (Cicirelli, 1995; Edwards et al., 2006). The depth of the relationship suggests they may remain a crucial source of emotional or material support when adults. Siblings bring their own expectations and obligations as intra-generational (Peletz, 1995: 350). In addition, anthropologists would expect considerable cultural variation in these expectations and obligations. For example, in some countries such as the Philippines, there are clear age-graded hierarchies between older and younger siblings, while in others, such as Trinidad, less so. As with parenting, this is clearly an arena of strong tensions and conflicting desires (Trawick, 1990: 152).

Siblings in Trinidad generally maintain very close relationships. The term is ambiguous; children will regard as their siblings other children they grew up with in the same household, who may share only one parent, or have no biological connection. They thereby exemplify Carsten's (2010) concept of kinship constituted by practice. Living in family homes, they commonly share bedrooms up to until marriage or moving out of the home. They thereby exemplify a point often made for kinship in the Caribbean (Gonzalez, 1984; Miller, 1994: 136–43), that people prefer to feel they have some choice in relationships rather than merely following obligation, partly because obligations weigh quite heavily in acknowledged kin reciprocities. As a result, these relationships stand halfway between the previous discussion of parenting and our following discussion of friendship. One of the key tensions in the sibling relationship (even more so with cousins) is how far a given relationship is pitched between the presumption of an axiomatic obligation given by birth and obligations expressive of personal love and concern.

Either way, the sense of commitment can be extremely powerful. Annissa and Prakesh, for example, who are both in their mid thirties, still live in their parents' home, since their mother passed away five years earlier. They have a sister in Canada whom they use Skype with regularly, mainly to catch up and talk to their nephew, who is eight years old. These are classic instances of the use of webcam to maintain a sense of presence and connectedness. Sherlon moved to Toronto some years ago to study business. Six months later, his younger brother joined him and they lived together while they were studying. Sherlon remembers that time as one of the most fun he's ever had; they also lived in a student apartment together when they were studying at St Augustine's (the campus for the University of the West Indies in Trinidad). 'We accustomed to living together, and when he went up, it just brought back all these good times, we went to the same place, liming, going where you want, come back, it was fun.' When Sherlon finished and moved back to Trinidad, his brother found it a very different and difficult situation, not having him around anymore. Now they're on Skype almost every day, for a couple of hours and longer on the weekend. They try to keep their brotherly housemate dynamic by using webcam as company. 'We have it on most of the time, so when he's home, he would put on his webcam and I would put on mine and whenever we're there he'll be cooking and we'll be cooking and we'll be talking. I wouldn't say it's a routine, but it's convenient. It's for him. For me a bit, but mainly for him, it's cos he misses home.' For Sherlon and his brother, the brotherly relationship is best expressed not by speaking in depth but by spending so much time together on webcam.

In the case of Jules, we see the additional criterion of personal affinity. Jules has one older half-brother who's ten years older than him and lives in Miami. They haven't lived in the same city since Jules was nine and they have mostly kept in touch by phone until two years ago when Jules got his laptop. As well as checking in and making sure the other is okay, the main thing Jules and his brother share over webcam is their passion for music, composing and song writing. Jules is working part-time, performing in a band, and his brother is a producer, so they use webcam to workshop with each other. 'If he just have to hear something because I does sing too, I does record music, so if it is I have to sing piece of a song for him to hear, I could just use the webcam and show it, he could see I'm playing the guitar as well, or the keyboard, and he will see it live and stuff, just to get his comments, just to get his views on it.' Jules' brother has a wife and a small daughter in Miami, so it's unlikely he will move back to Trinidad, so for Jules, music as the common interest allows them to spend time together, rather than just talking.

A similar situation may arise from shared business interests. In the past, this was often siblings bonded by common inheritance of agricultural land. Suni, a successful, middle-aged professional, runs his own consultancy business and uses webcam primarily to speak with his brother in Montreal. Webcam allows them to catch up and check on each other's health. They both own several properties and Suni will bring his laptop and show his brother any developments or renovations in his apartments, but also take the webcam to show his own large plot of land with the animals and him cutting his own corn in his yard.

In contrast to such brothers' more instrumental bonding, sisters may place more emphasis on conversation. Tenika uses webcam as her means to provide support for her brother studying in London. Tenika is the oldest daughter and her brother, the third child, is eight years younger. He keeps in contact with the wider family, but it's still Tenika he opens up to the most:

> There was an occasion where he was at university and I think he was having, he went through a period where he was having a really rough time just keeping up, speaking to him on the phone, he was like 'yeah everything's alright' you know, and how I knew there was a problem and he'll be like 'yeah I mean, you know it's cool, everything's alright' on the phone, but then I was talking to him on Skype and I was just looking at him and seeing sadness, and I said 'what's going on? You need to tell me what is really going on? Because I know something is going on and I don't know what it is and I'm looking at you and I'm seeing that you're struggling.' He got really emotional and then it ended up that he was kinda flunking out of school, you know, and it was a really rough time for him, but I knew. I didn't do much of the advising, I was more there to listen, because I think he felt that he really could not say all the things that he really wanted to say, to anybody else and it was just like my big sister, I could tell my big sister, you know.

Kendra

This focus on conversation and emotional support is even stronger when we look to purely female sibling relationships, as in the case of Kendra, whose twin sister Lenora moved to study in Jamaica last year. Up until then, they lived together, in the same room in their parents' house and had never been apart longer than a week. They speak on the phone every day, and they will Skype for a couple of hours once a week, where their conversations revolve around Lenora missing home, mutual stress about their university studies, checking in to see how the other one is and venting about what's going on in their lives. Kendra and Lenora are clearly very close, exhibiting what locally would be seen as many typical features of female siblings, a mixture of competition, rivalry, affection and care. Sometimes, they slip into an earlier mode of private conversation. Lenora adopts a high-pitched baby voice with a slight whinge and lisp guaranteed to irritate and wind Kendra up, who then takes on a parent's voice and reprimands her. They both have a fierce sense of humour, but it's clear that Lenora is the dominant twin. Living apart at university, Kendra has become more reflective of herself as an individual. She recognizes that she is quiet and doesn't like to appear too vulnerable, a trait she ascribes to having always taken a backseat to her more dominant twin when together in social interactions. When they speak on Skype, Kendra and Lenora will still playfully banter as well as indulge in long deep discussions about their own lives, mutual friends and kin.

When Kendra and Lenora argue, it's loud, with a good deal of gesticulation, pointing and standing tall. Without fail though, unless it is about something that Kendra believes so strongly in that she cannot back down, she will eventually give way: 'Generally, the way our arguments go, if we arguing about something, she tends to dominate the conversation and if I be loud, she tends to loud me down more often than not she loud me down.' However, on Skype, Kendra feels she doesn't have to remain in such confrontations, which she finds stressful.

> On Skype, she will loud me down and I will say 'well you know what, I don't really want to talk about this, I will talk to you later,'

> click. As opposed to like I think if she was really here, I think the argument would go much longer as we in each other's presence, and she will keep talkin talkin and eatin at me, and I will just have to retaliate, as opposed to where I can just say I really don't want to have this conversation and just close it off. So I think when we mad at each other and we on Skype, it does help, as you get to vent that to the other person . . . We don't come to a solution or anything like that, we will just 'well if that what you think', click. And maybe later on, we actually call on the phone, and then sort it out. But for some reason, when the tension is there now and you're seein the person, and a real argument happenin, for me I just won't, I don't like it. So I will just click and get outta that as fast as.

They know they can resolve these by phone or Skype when they have cooled down.

The case of Kendra and Lenora is closer to the given bonds we found in parenting. As a result, webcam seems to come in again as something that can both exacerbate and alleviate tensions. In this case, the combination of separation and Skype has allowed the twins to re-cast their relationship on a more equal and mature plane, as the technology has played to Kendra's desire to limit and delineate conflict. Being separated was certainly a challenge; they missed each other terribly, but with webcam they have reconnected as two more autonomous individuals and this has allowed them to become on balance closer and more supportive than when things were unremittingly co-present. Lenora is now home for her school holidays after her first year of living away. She and Kendra know that it's a temporary stay and they have found their relationship over the last month to be more like friends, where they have shared interests and they are getting to spend time together as individual personalities as well as sisters. Here we can see an alignment between our theory of attainment and that of kinship, in that the technology allows them to come much closer to what they both would have imagined to be the ideal relationship between siblings. Perhaps this is particularly clear because they are twins. These changes are also characterized as a movement from the sense of given obligations to a more voluntaristic sense of choosing to be close in the manner of best friends.

Friends

The anthropological and sociological literatures on friendship generally agree on three dimensions. Firstly, friendship is recreational: individuals use their spare time to spend together; secondly, friendship is a type of relationship that is built on choice and autonomy, where the relationship is nurtured by individuals; and thirdly, friendship is a key site for self-identification and development and it teaches us and shows us how to view ourselves (Allan, 1989; Bell and Coleman, 1999; Pahl, 2000). Friendship is also highly contextual and may pertain only to certain contexts such as work or education, and movement between social settings may disrupt the exchange within friendships (Carter, 2008). In the longer term, such friendships may evolve as following migration, where friendship networks become crucial as knowledge-based and support networks (Conradson and Latham, 2005). For anthropologists, there will always be the additional stress upon cultural variability in the meaning of friendship.

Within polymedia, face-to-face webcam follows on from the traditional phone conversation as relying on synchronic presence. Skype represents a request for, or a present of, time in a way that would not be true of email or Facebook. In her study of the virtual community Cybertown, Carter shows how this 'gift of time' becomes important in generating trust, intimacy and disclosure in an online context (2008). This factor is especially important when webcam is maintaining transnational communication, as this may require a sustained effort by one or other to deal with inconvenient times that may clash with work or other commitments. This aligns webcam with the first criterion of friendship as shared time, building from the school-based peer experience as kids who hang out together. This usually also means making shared time synchronic with other activities. Often, friendships had begun through using webcam while studying, having to complete the same assignment and sharing the sense that 'we are all in the same boat'. Leanda, who is studying for her Master's in Biochemistry, mainly works in her student apartment, but is logged onto Skype. 'I would have my friends on, with video and voice and we would be doing work and if I need to ask any questions, I'll just talk it out. It's also much more efficient to chat with my colleagues about work instead of typing, we could chat and discuss work while doing something else.'

Friends recognize that they distract each other, which is sometimes a problem but also provides the requisite breaks that help maintain efficient working. Leanda notes of her study partner, 'While I'm doing the work, he will do work as well, he's just there to answer questions and sometimes he'll be helping me out with my slides. We try to stay focused because we spend a lot of time in school, talking about other personal things.' Many students felt that webcam thereby combined some functional purpose with the desire to keep company. Avinash, who only finished high school last year, noted that:

> When I'm studying I'll be there with a friend [online] and if we need to talk about something then I'll probably just hail him out or shout out, something like that. You could always ask for a reference and their opinion on something, and with my style of learning and revising work, it's more comfortable to actually have somebody to talk to me than I read, because I don't really like to read, when you talk out stuff I think you actually remember it better as well.

These school and college uses of webcam can then migrate to a more general sense of hanging out with friends online, as in the case of Whitney.

Whitney

Hanging out together has a particular inflection for Trinidadians because the term 'liming', or 'to lime', remains central to national identity. Once a more street-corner or location-based form of mainly male sociality (Lieber, 1981), it now connotes almost any kind of hanging out together, though ideally including spontaneity and movement, such as driving around picking up more friends, or meeting at one house and then drifting on to another. Whitney suggests that her group have found ways to inject something of the quality of a lime, such as spontaneity and open-endedness, into webcam, despite the constraints. With her friends it's

> [b]ecause everybody's present, everybody's at home when we're on the webcam so one person would be like 'ok let me get something

> to eat' and the another person would say 'alright well since you're doing that, I'll go get something to eat too' and then another person would say 'well since everybody doing that, I'll go fix up something too' and we'll be talking and eating, it's just as if all of us are around the table now and we order something, we're eating, we're drinking, so we're like what are you eating and what are you eating and oh I wish I could have that now.

Such longer-term friendships develop very similar concerns to kin relationships. Whitney and her friends provide emotional support and counsel for any of them who's going through a difficult time:

> Mostly when any of us have some problem and we don't know what path to take, we'll message somebody and we'll meet and we'll talk about it. Because you're not there physically to console the person, the most you can say is try not to take it on or everything will work out. As opposed to if you were here, I would rub your back or I'll give you a hug, I'll get tissues for you to use, yeah it's not like that. I believe one hundred percent because in order for you to get the message across the way you want to get it across verbally and you can't do it emotionally, you need to use certain words and you need to impress on the person, you know, 'hey don't worry' and it depends on your tone of voice as well, so it's like you're caressing them with words. Sometimes I feel guilty, because I have all this work to do and I didn't call Casey or Marsha, two weeks ago I got an email from Marsha sayin 'you alive? We have so much to catch up on' because it's the time, it's not permitting and it's the time of year right now where we have end of term exams, but they understand, they've been through it.

Webcam is not necessarily part of building more intense relationships. Others used Skype simply to continue friendships with people they had once studied together with, but had now left Trinidad. Alongside Facebook, this may mean retaining a relationship they might otherwise have lost. The additional visual component of webcam helped appraise them of the new circumstances within which their friends were living: who they were sharing with, the kind of accommodation, whether their friend was dressed for cold weather or hot. Sometimes, where their previous studying together meant they had ended up working in the same or similar professions, such as teaching, webcam allows them to talk more deeply about their respective work experiences.

In his development of a sociological approach to friendship, Allan (1989) suggests that friends also become a resource of support outside of the family, whether it's practical support, as we have seen with Leanda's and Avinash's experiences as students, material or financial support or moral support. Close friends who use webcam to speak with each other frequently describe this communication in terms of an emotional bond that often intensified to compensate for the physical distance between them. The way in which they describe such relationships seems to bring us full circle back to the kinds of material we encountered earlier when talking about parents and siblings, as is evident in our final case of Jamie.

Jamie

Jamie works in a small gift shop which she runs with her father. During the day, she keeps her Notebook on the counter, where she is connected to Skype and Facebook. She often chats to her childhood best friend Ann who lives in New York and, around once a week, she will Skype her in the evenings when they have some privacy. She sees herself as providing the primary support for Ann, who, being away from home, is going through a more difficult time.

Jamie is extremely outgoing, and one of the things she likes about working in the store is that she knows and can chat with most of the people who come in. It gets a bit boring during those hours when customers are few and her sons are in school, so the Notebook allows her to stay by the counter while playing Farmville or chatting on Skype. She sometimes also uses Skype to make video calls while at work, but only when it's very quiet and the person really wants to speak with her. Otherwise, she would prefer to be at home, where she can give her undivided attention. Jamie is extremely close to Ann; their mothers went to school together and up until their late teenage years, they were always at each other's houses. Ann had relatives in New York, so 11 years ago she decided to move there to work. She has had Skype for the last two years. Before that, they always spoke by phone, never sending emails or letters because they would always have too much to say. Yet comparing the phone to Skype, Jamie reflects on how boring it was, they would be using phone cards and talk out the time, squeezing in as much as they could. 'Now at least, she sees my sons, I see her kids, they get to talk to me, I get to talk to them.'

Moreover, using Skype has allowed Jamie to feel like she's able to give genuine support to Ann:

> She kinda cries a lot too eh, so she get emotional. It's sad because knowing that she's far away, we cannot do all the stuff that we used to growing up and her life is totally different, where she have to take care of her children by herself. She left her job because her elder child's dad, he used to work there, that's where she met him, and she had a personal issue with him because he's married and she had a child with him, so she's going through it where she having the wife nagging her and throwing and calling her and she talk to me personally through Skype. And I say, 'Yuh made a mistake, but yuh have to look at it future wise, not for now.' So when I speak to her that way, that's the best I can do for her.

Jamie often speaks to Ann in a mix of stern and concerning voice because she feels she has to make use of what the medium can offer – Ann can see her. For Jamie, there is no use crying and sharing her pain; she would prefer to be a support to her friend by using her face to show how strong and useful her advice is, because, she says, it comes from her own experience. 'I can't you know, send a hug, but I can encourage her to do better.' With Skype, Jamie feels more able to transcend the problems of distance and time differences, to retain her position as Ann's critical support, also allowing webcam to take up what seems a natural role as a kind of digital 'confessional' to Ann. In turn, it works as a form of technological podium for Jamie. In that sense, webcam becomes a remediation of quite traditional genres in such supportive relationships that being familiar are also more comfortable. But these are also transformations that would have worked equally well in the discussion of core parenting and sibling relationships.

Conclusion

Looking across the range of relationships presented here, we can see a spectrum from kin relations based on obligations given by birth, to the more voluntaristic choices expressed by friendship.

Indeed, perhaps the widest generalization from these Trinidadian case studies is to suggest that webcam facilitates the transition of kinship into more friendship-like modes as children become adults, while equally facilitating a drift for some long-term friendships into something more like the deep concern and emotional support of kinship, although, no doubt, there are many exceptions.

These transformations take on a particular significance in Trinidad. In Miller's (1994) earlier analysis of kinship in Trinidad, he argued that the traditions of structured kinship come into conflict with powerful idioms of freedom. In the Caribbean, the history of slavery and indentured labour had created a latent resentment about ever being merely taken for granted within any kind of relationship, implying that one should always be free to opt out. For example, one of the reasons many Trinidadians traditionally avoided marriage until late into a relationship was that marriage seemed to institutionalize the idea of taking one's partner for granted. After the traumas of slavery and indentureship, the ideal of freedom was palpable and something to be preserved even within intimate relationships. In this chapter, we can see how even siblingship expresses this tension. Kendra and Lenora were always intensely close as sisters, but now have managed to re-configure this as something they choose rather than the mere obligation of kin roles. This allows them to feel even closer. As such, webcam is becoming insinuated within one of the most important points of contradiction within Trinidadian relationships.

Once again we can see how, as in our theory of attainment, the position of webcam is largely given by the tensions and contradictions that it appears, at least at first, to help resolve. Of course, it is very likely that it will in turn produce its own such tensions. In the very same chapter we have the example of Emily's father. This is just as much a case of attainment as that of Kendra and Lenora. Emily's father has attained a new relationship with his daughter. He thoroughly dislikes it, and experiences it as a failure, creating considerable anxiety. He has lost what he considered to be valuable in his role as father. But that is not the point; he has still attained this worse relationship through the use of webcam.

Three things come together here as one might expect in a work of anthropology. There is a series of general academic debates about kinship as, for example, in the difference between Carsten and Miller on how far behaviour becomes constitutive of a particular kinship role such as fatherhood. But when returned to the ethnography, this general debate becomes a more specific issue for Trinidad because the degree of voluntarism in kinship relationships is at a premium, following the history of slavery and indentured labour. Into such complex situations arrives webcam, which as attainment seems to both resolve some tensions and exacerbate others. More specifically, this chapter has shown that the experience of webcam is at first almost always the other side of a coin to the experience of separation, leading to our emphasis on retention and maintenance. Surprisingly often, people seemed to feel that after considered reflection, this dual experience of webcam/separation corresponded to a maturing of a relationship because it creates conditions for the proper degree of autonomy. Finally, we should also note examples that look more like pure retention or maintenance of what otherwise would have been lost relationships, as in the facility of webcam to reconnect elderly grandparents with their grandchildren.

The literature on friendship tends to already focus on issues of choice, recreation and self-development, marking a strong contrast with the anthropological study of kinship, which began as an analysis of order and structure. By juxtaposing the two, we have hoped to introduce a more nuanced and humanistic sense, especially of kinship as experience. We have also emphasized the degree to which any impact of webcam builds upon the prior trajectories of relationships. For example, the way peer group circles formed at school can develop, incorporating elements of the local idiom of 'liming' and then evolve into deeper concerns with emotional support. We see webcam inserted into the entire spectrum from the most structured relationships of parenting, to the least structured of friendship, and as an instrument that helps different kinds of relationship flow between these two poles.

6

Polymedia

Introduction: polymedia as theory

The term 'polymedia' was coined recently by Madianou and Miller (2012a, 2012b) for two reasons. The first was that there was simply no current terminology to describe the contemporary situation in which most people in developed countries have access to both a phone with a pre-paid contract and a computer. This has meant that the traditional reasons for choosing any one particular media for an act of communication, that is either access or cost, no longer applied. One can equally well text, speak, BBM, see, Facebook or email. As a result, any individual act of communication has become costless at the point of selection. As a result, we are not looking so much at a choice between media, as the particular configuration of different media that an individual deploys.

The term 'polymedia' is intended to address the consequences as well as the acknowledgement of these changes. It was proposed that this represents an effective re-socializing of communications media. If the grounds for choosing a media or the way people configured their combination of media was no longer based upon access or cost, then the reasons people choose, and even more importantly, the reasons others would impute to their choices, were now presumed by others to be social and moral (e.g., Gershon, 2010). With this new freedom of choice comes responsibility for one's selections, which can be judged as evidence for our character made evident to others. So apart from proposing a new term to describe the emerging environment of proliferating communication opportunities, Madianou and Miller were proposing polymedia as a social theory of media. In general, neologisms are best avoided, but in this case it seems warranted since there is no colloquial word for these profound changes.

Polymedia also represents an essential point with respect to a book on webcam, which otherwise would constitute an artificial extraction of this one particular media from the context in which it is always a decision to use Skype as against, or in combination with, other media. No one just uses Skype. We need to re-engage webcam within its wider media ecology (Slater and Tacchi, 2004), which also differs from region to region. For example, we shall see how the BlackBerry phone has a particular resonance in Trinidad, not found in London. This in turn gives webcam a slightly different inflection as either combined with, or as an alternative to, a BlackBerry. As in the traditions of structural anthropology, we can only understand webcam by focusing upon what it is not, i.e., the alternatives that might have been selected, as well as what it is. Towards the end of this chapter, we shall also look at one of the most interesting qualities of a platform such as Skype, which is that it also represents a form of polymedia internally. Skype is not just webcam. On Skype, one can simultaneously speak, see and text people. This turns out to have interesting implications, so Skype represents an internal as well as external issue of polymedia.

An anthropological approach to polymedia needs to acknowledge the particular trajectories of each individual medium; for example, the evolution of texting in the Philippines (Madianou and Miller, 2012a) or the particular trajectory Facebook has taken in Trinidad (Miller, 2011). The concept of remediation (Bolter and Grusin, 2000) has been particularly helpful, as it emphasizes the degree to which any new media is embryonically formed, in light of the media that precede it; for example, how television at first used the idioms of radio.

Polymedia also builds upon earlier concepts such as technological convergence and media ecology that recognized how each medium finds its niche with respect to all the others (Slater and Tacchi, 2004; Jenkins, 2006; Horst et al., 2010; Ito, 2010). For anthropologists, this ecology should include not only other media, but also the wider social systems or infrastructures, such as family, transport, health and government (see Slater and Tacchi, 2004; Horst and Miller, 2006). Prior to the concept of polymedia, one of the most important ways the relationship between media has been conceptualized is in terms of affordances (see Hutchby, 2001). This term indicates the propensities that any media has for particular kinds of usage. This is something that has been particularly well explored by two recent volumes: that of Baym (2010) in the larger field of personal connections using digital media, and Broadbent (2011) from her extensive empirical study of media use within Swiss families. Both exemplify the study of different media as complementary to each other.

Baym (2010) cuts the cake according to what she regards as key parameters of difference, properties that may be shared or make for significant contrasts among these new media. Seven are highlighted: kinds of interactivity, temporal structure, social cues, storage, replicability, reach and mobility (Baym, 2010: 6–12). Baym employs these key concepts to consider a wide range of facets of human communication, including the degree to which we see media as more or less authentic in comparison to face-to-face interaction, the sense of community, identity, gender, veracity and the self. Broadbent also identified various key elements behind the choice of particular media, such as 'privacy, discretion, needing immediate feedback, availability of the communication partner, frequency of conversations, familiarity, or formality of the relationship' (Broadbent, 2011, translation courtesy of author). Broadbent's main focus is upon which media are more or less demanding of attention, something which would shift dramatically between face-to-face webcam and 'always-on' webcam, as well as misunderstandings that arise in the formation of norms such as gendered usage.

In their initial discussion of polymedia, Madianou and Miller (2012a, 2012b) stress the implications of this new combinatorial capacity of media for issues such as the communication and control of emotions, and also power and asymmetries within relationships. Both of these will be prominent topics within this chapter. The point is that the configuration of these various media is not so much an expression of an individual and their identity, but rather the relationship between the two individuals communicating. As such, this chapter continues the work of previous chapters in showing how the emergence of this configuration of media contributes to relationship dynamics.

Cost

It follows that we can only properly concern ourselves with the issues of polymedia to the degree that we can argue that cost and access have become largely eliminated as the grounds for choice in the manner now found throughout the developed countries. It would clearly not be appropriate for the situation in much of Africa (Burrell, 2012; Wyche et al., 2013). Yet, it is becoming more relevant to parts of South East Asia such as Cambodia and Vietnam (Bernhardt and Milberg, 2011). Trinidad has oil money and a fine tradition of education, but standards of living are well below those of the UK and there are areas of quite dire poverty. So we would seem open to criticism if we failed to properly address something that 'must' be a factor. But we prefer to follow the tenor of our evidence. Take, for example, an interview with a social worker living in the poorest area of El Mirador. The welfare net in Trinidad is quite restricted and to be part of her constituency, a client had to show evidence of severe deprivation to qualify for state aid. Yet, she had no provision for contacting clients other than through mobile phones, the presumption being that such phones are now ubiquitous irrespective of destitution in all other respects. Furthermore, she reported that her clients were increasingly using webcam. While they could not afford computers, they found ways of gaining access through family members, neighbours, friends and internet cafés. Other contributing factors are that for the past three years, all primary school children in the country have been provided with free laptops with webcam, and El Mirador has become increasingly provisioned with public access Wi-Fi hotspots. The social worker also confirmed our impression that, given the nature of families in the island, any computer in the house is assumed to be the joint possession of all. It was clear that this social worker no longer saw cost and access as significant factors in communication and thereby presumed polymedia for all. A digital divide perspective would be an unwarranted imposition by us as academics rather than something emergent from ethnography. So we will presume polymedia. By contrast, factors of inequality remain highly pertinent to Trinidadians' use of polymedia, which is why power will be a focus of this chapter.

One reason for being cautious about concepts such as 'affordances' is that often the key elements of media usage come more from happenstance than anything that could be called given propensities of that media. As pointed out in several sections of this book, the study of webcam must always begin from the sheer absurdity that adding the additional dimension of sight, so far from adding to cost, was coincidental with replacing a costly media – the phone – with one – Skype – that was free at the point of usage. What kind of affordance is it where giving access to the visual reduces instead of adds to cost? But that previous experience of the phone as expensive could remain associated with the device. In Miller's current study of terminal cancer patients in England, some older patients have never really forgiven the phone for its legacy of expense, and as a result have never managed to be at ease in its company. They remain tense and time conscious even though the cost plans have changed.

Remediation

Innovations are always first understood in terms of past trajectories. The concept of remediation (Bolter and Grusin, 2000) seems most appropriate when one can see how a new medium is forged in the image of a predecessor. For example, it helps to understand the use of webcam at Christmas in the light of the established traditions of sending Christmas cards. The Christmas card is quite a distinct category within the universe of cards. It had accrued the sense of obligation, a minimal unit of sociability, where it could be the sole remaining evidence of a social contact. Even if you did nothing the rest of the year, sending a Christmas card acknowledged that this remained a latent connection that could be reactivated at some point. For some informants, while they would also use webcam more generally, there was already developing a 'tradition' of Christmas family webcam, which is the only occasion during the year when the two extended families become present to each other as such. One entire family would simultaneously webcam another entire family using two or more webcams, depending on where they were living, exchanging greetings family to family. Some had tried Christmas e-cards, which at first seem a closer analogy to the traditional offline cards, but these don't seem to have been satisfying. Group webcam could replace the card because it added to, rather than subtracted from, that tradition.

What helped webcam occupy this niche was a combination of being more recent, i.e. the latest thing, and its addition of an extra sensory dimension as the visual, both of which gave it the aura of 'special' and therefore was suited to marking special events. This applied not just to Christmas, but to other important acts of communication: 'yeah, it's not like a regular everyday thing, like you go on Facebook every day. It's like you go on Skype when you really have something important to tell somebody.' Similarly, the meaning of Skype derives in part from the particular way it emerges from another medium. For example, a person remarks about her contacts that on 'MSN I have two hundred and something I think, and on Skype, I think about thirty-something. Everybody on Skype is people I know personally, on MSN it just have people who might see me on Facebook and just add me, but on Skype I only have people who I actually know, like actual real friends and family.' She is being more circumspect with this more recent medium, having allowed an older media, MSN, to become too generic.

These historical trajectories have a quality of serendipity because there is no technical reason why, for example, Skype would have more or fewer people connected through it than MSN. At other times, people would legitimate their particular form of polymedia using terms that are closer to the concept of affordance. Media use is defended according to what they are differentially 'good for', in the manner described by Baym or Broadbent. This was especially true of commercial and office contexts, where there is a premium on rationalizing choice. For example, an office worker says, 'And if you're doing other things at the same time they can see if your focus is a hundred per cent or not. Whereas on the phone you could keep your focus while you're doing something else. But then to be seen they might think they don't have your full attention.'

There is, however, a constant blurring of technical and cultural aspects of affordances, where the term 'culture' stands for a multitude of quite different contextual features. It sounds like a cultural generality when someone says that they see Facebook as more populated by college kids, or that for Trinidadians, BlackBerry is addictive. But it can also be the way groups categorize each other with respect to what they see as properties of each medium. A woman might generalize when she claims she uses the phone for relatives, but Skype with her close girlfriends, because she feels comfortable joking around with the latter, an informality she assumes comes with Skype. Yet, other people might regard Skype as more formal when sitting in front of a desktop computer, but informal when using a mobile medium such as a smartphone or laptop. The result of these ambiguities and the mash-up of reasons given for choices of media is that most individuals now acknowledge not just a wide spectrum of media, but an equally wide spectrum of legitimations, rationalizations and even perceptions of what each medium adds to their own mix within personal communication. What we end up with is a litany of matches between the different media choices and the grounds for their selection as in:

> Say writing on people's walls. I will do that very rarely, and I will message people, but you know how people post for people to see, I don't really do that. If I want to tell you something, I will send you a message. I don't want the whole world to know what this is. I will send it directly to you. And yeah, I do text a lot. I use the phone a good bit too. I definitely use long emails, like to the friend who is not here. At least the most juicy communication that takes place between us, is in long email. Even just recently she tell meh – I have a drama to tell you. I tell her on Facebook, I am waiting, I'm impatient, and she tell meh and she send meh a long email . . . My email is predominantly for that and work and study kinda thing . . . I may have boxed myself in the first instance in that particular way, because I preferred email, I felt safer sending you an email and I felt it wasn't too intrusive on my time, my space. So if it's convenient, I'll email you, you email me and sometimes the most trivial of things. It's convenient, but it offers something different. For example to converse with Skype, it's an immediate thing and I see you. I'm actually hearing you at the moment and I can respond at the moment, which makes it much more interesting depending on what you're talking about, because I'm not going to talk to you about a movie on Skype. I want to see you face to face

> to talk about personal life issues. I can understand and appreciate how other people use it for that, but for me, it takes away from the intimacy that I appreciate in communicating with people. If the person is abroad or something like that then I'll be flexible, but I still prefer a phone call. Yes I prefer putting the phone to my ear or writing you a letter. I love writing letters, so the transition from the letters would have been the email.

Polymedia is rarely tidy. We see that sometimes the issue is how effective a medium is seen to be, at other times how it grew out of a previous medium. But, often, it's hard to ascribe more than personal preferences to such discussion. Having this stream of description is rather overwhelming, but sometimes it is still possible to distil from discussion, or from knowing more about an individual, how their personal configuration of media has evolved and how it makes sense to them. Our example comes from a man we shall call Christian.

Christian

For Christian, the relationship to webcam takes on a more polymedia aspect within the workplace. Webcam at work may be Skype, but equally it may come through Facebook, Yahoo, Googlechat or MSN. He might send a photo through BBM and then Skype to discuss the issue. When busy, he will message. When people can't synchronize, he may send a voicemail. But for conference calls between people on the various islands, he likes Skype. He regards it as simple and saves money. As with many people today, media is a form of layered sandwich that develops naturally with his daily experience of computer use. So both Gmail and Skype come on automatically when he turns on his computer. He describes these two as his 'bread and butter'. The next layer is likely to be Facebook, there in the background. While the filling and the pickles are made up by a mix of whatever other programs he will turn on as need arises, none of them are automatic. All of these are constantly accompanied by the ubiquity of BlackBerry off screen like a plate of chips. The BlackBerry on the side has a special place because 'like I can send a message while I'm in a crowded room and it doesn't impact on anyone else, nobody can listen to what you're saying, I can be talking to you and I can be on the phone sending messages and it wouldn't impact on what we're doing here'. It means whatever else is happening, there is another channel that can be having its own little conversation:

> My co-workers, if it is they're running late, they can just send me a BBM or an email to the entire IT team, instead of having to call individually. Webcam fits in as a more serious engagement or consultancy. So that if the user has a problem, the user could be chatting with me and explaining to me the nature of the problem, instead of me going out there and not knowing what to expect, I can get a better idea what the problem is while still being here and troubleshooting what the problem is without having to move from here.

By contrast, he refuses to use Facebook as something with similar potential in relation to work, since for him Facebook is employed as an entirely social media that keeps work and work relationships bracketed off.

Christian is entirely capable of being simultaneously a conscientious IT officer who wants to keep as many channels open in order to effectively carry out his work. But, he is also a sensitive young man who wants to make sure that he is not neglecting his social obligations. There is nothing of that social dysfunctional 'geek' about him that people sometimes ascribe to workers such as IT officers. On the contrary, the key to understanding his use of polymedia is the way media helps him resolve some of the contradictions of living a hectic modern life that remains sensitive to social as well as work demands. For example, he knows that being so busy with his work leads various relatives to feel they are being ignored. But he has found that five minutes with a webcam makes them feel they are getting some real attention in a way that surpasses any other media's ability to express this genuine interest in them. At the very same time, the fact that he is using webcam which is on his computer, unlike, for example, a phone, also means that actually he is making this powerful social statement while simultaneously remaining within his core work environment, on his computer, where everything else is going on. He will achieve this either through using a split screen on a single monitor, or have several monitors around: 'So it really assists you in that way in terms of multi-tasking, whereas if you're holding a phone, unless you're on a headset, you don't have your hands free like that.' He can both split his attention while apparently giving more attention to a single person at the same time. This is not a deceit, but merely using the new capacities of the media to simultaneously work better and socialize better. In fact, the one thing that is sacrificed is self-regard. He is one person who barely notices the image of himself on the screen, which holds no interest for him.

Polymedia also helps resolve personal issues of constantly working but also needing a companion's presence:

> Sometimes, especially if you're up late and you have work to do and you're sitting down home, someone can go 'ehh I'll keep you company' and stuff like that. And it helps to have someone, a presence there. So even though they're not physically there, they're still there, they'll talk to you every now and again, and it's not like they're communicating right through, but they can drop you a line 'how's it going', 'yuh makin any progress so far', 'let me read it' you know. So these little things appear and stuff and you can send it to them. They can review it and send it back to you and give their input. So that little interaction really helps you as well.

Christian's personal configuration of media has in turn to adapt to the other people he is in contact with, and he compromises accordingly. There is a stark contrast in his relationship to his father and to his mother, for example. His father, at 57, remains constantly at work, wielding two BlackBerrys. Like his son, he manages a host of clients as a bank procurement officer but retains a commitment to Skyping his sisters in the US. Christian's father, like Christian, argues that BBM manages to be both a highly efficient way to work, and more personal as a relationship to clients and customers. By contrast, his mother has never really taken to any of the new media; there is a kind of internal family digital divide in that respect. The image is of her cooking and cleaning as a housewife, picking her way amongst her husband's laptops, tablets, PCs, phones and all the rest of his digital detritus that messes up her home. When she calls Christian, it is as much a reminder that there are still some people who use a house phone. So he would prefer to drive 15 minutes and spend time with her and recognize that she regards all the rest of this stuff as just a nuisance.

This could be described as a portrait of Christian. Although we will need to look at wider social normativity in understanding polymedia, this description of Christian shows that polymedia can also be a means for describing an individual. We have learnt a great deal about the qualities of the man. That he is ingenious, but also highly sensitive to his social commitments, including their potential for loneliness and their need for company. He does something that theorists often neglect, which is to appreciate that often morality can be achieved effectively through efficiency rather than by repudiating functionality. The result is polymedia as an individual configuration, where the mix of media is also constitutive of the personality of the user.

The BlackBerry connection

The example of Christian emphasizes the way polymedia implicates a particular configuration of media at the level of the individual. But as an anthropological investigation, we need to set this, in turn, within wider cultural trajectories and generalities. Since the evidence in this book is dominated by our Trinidadian fieldwork, it seems sensible to balance the discussion so far with an example of a more specifically Trinidadian inflection to polymedia. There is no particular resonance to the BlackBerry phone in Australia or the UK, from where we come. Its previous associations were more with commercial interests. But in Trinidad, we soon came to appreciate that understanding webcam depends upon first taking a much more respectful stance towards the BlackBerry, which is the foundation for many Trinis' relationship to new media. For Trinidadians, the BlackBerry is treated like an entirely different sub-species within media ecology from phones or even smartphones. The analysis which follows pertains to the period 2010–12. By 2013, however, the BlackBerry was in decline against more fashionable smartphones, though the phone application WhatsApp had allowed some of the qualities of BBM, the characteristic BlackBerry messenger service, to migrate to these other phones, and if anything these points about BlackBerry are becoming still more pertinent as they hold also for WhatsApp, which has copied many of the traits of BBM.

The question of what makes a BlackBerry 'Trinidadian' is best answered by a Trinidadian:

> Well it's a smartphone, it doesn't affect your work, it's always there. One of the things I like is that you could see when a message is delivered and when it's read by the person. So you know that the person saw the message and if they chose to respond or not, and they could do it at any time. You could do a lot of things through BBM, send files, pictures, music, share files, once it's on your phone, it's simple. Probably like three or four different people in a day, but I have almost fifty-something contacts. So yeah, my girlfriend and one of my friends who lives close by and one or two co-workers who have a BlackBerry. So I kinda chat with them. I used to work in Head Office and about six people there had a Black-Berry and we all added each other. So at some point in the day we'll BBM each other. Gossip or typical work stuff, well mostly it was actual work, and everybody is close with each other, nobody has any beef with one another so it's normal shit talk. But some-times you're out of the office and you try to call someone and you can't get through, so you BBM someone to tell them call you, things like that.
>
> Sometimes they may be busy, because sometimes they read the message but they don't respond right away, they may respond later on in the day. So you know that they saw the message but they just can't respond, because it's one thing to see the message but it's another thing to type it out. Sometimes it does have some people that actually saw and just doesn't reply and when you ask them about it they're like 'I see it there yuh know but I just forget.' Sometimes people does be so busy they just forget to reply.
>
> The chats remain open, so if you have fifty contacts and you chat with each of them, you have a chat box, so all the chats remain open, it won't delete or anything. Is something like Facebook, you could update your status. It's not as defined as Facebook, where you could see your relationship status and you could see each other's friends, but it's more personalised . . . they just want the BBM, because if you have a BlackBerry, you just want the BBM because you know you could communicate with everybody else.

What comes across from this description is the Trinidadian empha-sis upon the relationship, and the constant anxiety about the state of any given relationship. The advantage of the BlackBerry is that you know when and if the other person has read the message that you sent. If they claim not to have seen it, you know that they lied. You know if they have responded immediately or delayed their response. There may be grounds for this; they could be busy, but at least you can tell. The flow is fairly constant between you and them. This is true for individual communication but also the BlackBerry allows for group chat and status updates such that it combines the ease of texting with the facilities of a social networking site. But it is this quality of responsiveness that aligns the BlackBerry with a key quality of polymedia, which is that it facilitates our ability to judge each other. With polymedia, we are judged on our choice of media. With BlackBerry, we are judged on the speed and nature of our response. How much concern have they shown for your message and what does that tell you about the immediate state of your relationship to them?

Behind this is a much wider argument Miller (1994) makes about the nature of Trinidadian ontology, that is the experience of being. He argues that Trinidadians tend to understand who they are largely in terms of the response of other people. Being is re-created by every responsive event rather than as a more lasting condition. They are able to reject institutionalized, hierarchical and categorical definitions of who they are by placing the emphasis on being constantly re-defined by others. The details of this argument are not germane here, but it shows how and why the BlackBerry might have found a niche within a relatively specific sense of what it is to be a person in Trinidad. This is helped by the fact that the BlackBerry is always with the person. There was an anxiety about having to find a computer to look at Facebook, for example. So it was also significant that it was the BlackBerry which became the main means by which people could keep Facebook on their person. When we started fieldwork, BlackBerry was already ubiquitous at least amongst younger Trinis with sufficient means. The BlackBerry handset was marketed with deep discounts in Trinidad as part of the company's desire to 'hook' this particular population. We would argue that was successful also because the phone found a niche that was ideal for Trinidadian sensibilities. As another person put it, 'It's like if you remember something right on the spot, it's like, "oh let me see if that person is on" or if you forgot something and you know one of your friends is going to be on their BlackBerry that time. You can pull out your

BlackBerry and ask them without having to call them or text them, it's a simple back and forth, back and forth.'

These arguments in turn explain a common observation of our informants which is that Trinidadians seem addicted to their BlackBerrys, evident in their inability to resist responding to the sound, a kind of 'ping', that tells them of a BBM message. This seems to be true despite whatever else is happening. Merely to mention this 'ping' sound causes laughter and embarrassment about the fact that people are helpless to refuse it. Yet, they don't feel the same imperative to answer any other kind of phone or respond to any other genre of message. One teacher talked of not answering her BBM while in the middle of teaching a class as though it was some kind of triumph of the will. But when the BlackBerry is understood as the medium which most fully equates with the Trinidadian concept of ontology, then this makes much more sense. Every BBM is a statement about the state of one's relationship to another person and thus a sign of who one actually is. It is better understood as analogous with the example taken from Flaubert in our first chapter – the heroine as a person who is constantly seeing mirrors as she walks from place to place and simply can't resist the opportunity to see how she looks at that moment, which also aligns this discussion of being with that chapter's concern with self-consciousness.

Having established what a BlackBerry is, within this particular context, we can now re-examine what webcam is through its relationship to the BlackBerry. For example, Christian noted that he uses Skype to make the other person feel special, that it gives them considerable attention and regard. But another Trini uses BlackBerry to achieve this effect in his relationship to his mother, who lives two miles 'down South'. 'So it's right there, I see her all the time, we work together. Yesterday she was in my apartment, had her make some sales calls, but we don't really need Skype.' Where Christian uses Skype as a kind of depth, a short burst of intensity, this Trini sees the BlackBerry as an alternative because it provides breadth that is a sense that they are constantly in touch throughout the whole day. But both are markers of their concern and attention.

Another 21-year-old Trini called Cindy found that her life was being completely taken over by the combination of her BlackBerry and Facebook:

> I lost to an extent the ability to communicate face to face, because everything would be – I'm just sitting here typin typin typin. But I think Skype and that webcam era was for us a means for us to communicate, to get back that interaction. Yeah. Because the same way I felt like I had to communicate to him with the camera, see how we are here, speaking now, it's the same kind of interaction without the physical presence, but the same interaction.

Cindy sees the use of these media as a kind of deterioration from true social communication, a nostalgic lament one hears far more often in London, but is present as a discourse in Trinidad. So for her, this quality of Skype as depth is still required despite the presence of BlackBerry as the breadth to this relationship.

These characters juxtaposed suggest there is a wide range of views as to what each medium represents, but what they have in common is a dialogue about the moral consequences of media selection (Gershon, 2010). If some swear by Facebook as an authentic expression of Trinidad, the next person claims it is the destruction of Trinidadian authenticity. People rarely sound neutral with regard to the place of the BlackBerry within Trinidad. It is either, as with Christian, something that saves their bacon, given the constant demands of modern life, or something they avoid like the plague, because it is a curse, an affliction or an addiction. With respect to webcam, moral judgement takes a slightly different turn, in that, as other chapters have shown, there is a sense of webcam as a purveyor of truth that brings one face to face with the actuality of the other. This leads us to more specific questions about polymedia as the vehicle of emotions and power.

Emotions and power

In writing about polymedia as a means to analyse their research materials from the Philippines, Madianou and Miller (2012a, 2012b) spend at least as much time on the content of what is communicated as on the choice of media. Issues of power were integral to their study of the changing dynamics of long distance mother–child relations. Questions of power obviously arise in this study of webcam, but seem more diffused given that we are not concentrating on any particular relationship. There is more consistency with regard to the other aspect of those mother–child relationships, the ability of different media to express emotions. Fortunately, the study of emotions becomes an effective, if vicarious, route to the consideration of power. This is because, so often, the issue with emotions is found to be one of control, ranging from self-control to control over the conversation to control over the other person.

The way emotions and power can be conflated comes out clearly in the case of Kendra, speaking about her twin Lenora, whom we met in the previous chapter:

> So for the most part if she arguing about something, and generally, the way our arguments go, if we arguing about something, she tends to dominate the conversation . . . and I will say 'well you know what, I don't really want to talk about this, I will talk to you later,' click. And maybe later on, we actually call on the phone, and then sort it out. But for some reason, when the tension is there now and you're seein the person, and a real argument happenin, for me I just won't, I don't like it. So I will just click and get outta that as fast as. It might be on the phone because you're not ready to see that person. So if you call meh on the phone and you like 'we need to talk about' then I'll be 'well maybe I Skype you tonight'. So the whole thing is diffused now and we can have a normal decibel level conversation then I can deal with that.
>
> There is often time a lull, which if it was on the phone, it might be better to deal with, cos you would pretend you get disconnected and hang up the phone. But with Skype, you can see the lull, but even though both parties can see the lull, you can both laugh it off easier cos if I'm on the phone I notice that when I'm talkin to my friend and there's a lull we will say how's school or how's study how's life or something like that. But if I'm talking on Skype and there's a lull, I might end up laughin and she will end up laughin, for some reason random things seem to come to your mind on Skype rather than on the phone when the lull is just there and you can't do anything about it. But yeah, there has been times when there will be a lull in the conversation and I would say 'So you have nuttin else to say or what?' and then you can joke about it. But if I'm on the phone with her, the lull is very . . . palpable. I can cope with the lull better on Skype than on the phone.

We noted this tension in the previous chapter between communicating with a person as exemplifying the category sibling and the character of one particular sibling. Similarly, one can hear beneath the surface of description the way people commonly shift register between how they are trying to judge their relationship with their specific girlfriend and how they tend to generalize about what *men* or *women* are 'like' when it comes to communication:

> Because what happens now is I have an expectation in the morning to wake up and to see a message from him or to call him on Skype or to get a message from him on Skype. And for me, that was a wake-up call for me, where I know I can tend to expect a lot, which would lead to disappointment in that he wouldn't do what I expect him to do. So me being conscious of that is good for me. You know, try to pull back on that engaging too much in communication to the extent that waking up every day, every day, every day and expect to see a call. But, it's just time and eventually whatever is meant to be will be. If he calls, he calls, if he doesn't, ok it's not a problem. To be ok with it, whereas before I was like 'why isn't he calling, why didn't I get a message, has something happened?' And get unnecessarily unnerved by the situation and yeah, it a wake-up call and a consciousness even for myself to know what weaknesses and what strengths I have in dealing with certain relationships.
>
> I'm a very emotional person, all the time. So like I would tend to try and filter so many things I would have to say or how I say it because I don't want to come across as too strong or too emotionally overbearing. For him, I don't really think he cares. For me, I know how emotional I can be so I try to limit it, at least for now, where I can express fully what I am trying to say without the additional emotion. But I don't want to think too much about the situation, I don't want to think because he calls me a lot or I call him and he responds, what's up with that? It doesn't necessarily mean anything. He just likes to talk, and I'm just a means for him to express himself. So I don't want to over think the situation, just because he callin me all the time, he like me, or he's committed to it or anything like that. I just want to let it be.

Evidently, the one thing this woman is never going to be able to do is simply 'just let it be'. Typically, the more significant the relationship, the more emotions, power and control become conflated. Looking across the range of our material, it becomes clear that most are not examples of power as a mode of domination and control. More commonly, we found both power and emotions being used as a means of showing sensitivity, care and concern for the other person.

For example, there is an established genre in gender relations where boyfriends, at least in new relationships, are seen as playing mind games by delaying their responses to texts from their girlfriends, leaving the latter in a state of frustrated anticipation. We found in Trinidad that rather than being put in that position of feeling obliged to give an immediate reply, men would often turn off their mobile phones and remain inaccessible. They saw this as preventing problems within the relationship, rather than trying to dominate. As academics, we are trained to look for power in its cruder form, and especially in gender relations, as though power is axiomatically a mode of oppression. We don't want to detract from whole swathes of oppressive and exploitative aspects of gender relations, but such assumptions can also become the complacency of academia. It then seems worth noting that in this case there was stronger evidence that people were trying to use webcam to achieve a strong sense of mutuality. For example, one of the most common grounds for favouring webcam is the idea that the person you love is holding back on everything that is wrong, which only becomes evident through webcam:

> I would say you're saying that but it's not like that. But if I'm seeing her I can say 'well yes, what is it that's wrong. Why is it you're not saying?' We could talk about it later or something like that, but yes. You can see that it is not right. It's not because of her that I would know that, I know by tone of voice, her expression yes, she's not somebody that expresses easily, but I can tell by tone of voice. How you see I would also pick up on that, it comes with knowing someone. We grew up together, I would know something is wrong, I would ask her 'why don't you tell me' and she would say 'you know I don't want to bother you.' And I would say 'tell me I want to know . . . She may not tell me on Skype, she's not as much into Skype, but she would tell me when she's on the phone and when she can go to a room alone.

It may be Skype where people find it easier to give way to their emotions or, as in this case, the phone. One of the advantages in thinking about polymedia is that it helps avoid the problems of overgeneralization about media. Most often, our informants position webcam as half way between the phone and face to face and therefore see it as more suited than the phone as a medium for expressing emotion directly to the other person. But there are plenty of people, as in the last example, for whom this is not true. Or, the issue of power and self-control means that the ease by which emotions break through on Skype is a reason to avoid it:

> I just don't go on Skype. When we get angry and stuff it's hard. Funny enough we also make up fast. We can't go a night without each other, so when we vexed for one night and by the morning, I'm so sorry da da da. Well I'll turn off my phone and I won't want to see Skype and then in the morning I'll turn on my phone and I'll have like a hundred emails saying I'm sorry da da da da. And I'll give in and then we get back together.

As previously noted, a problem can be that webcam creates an insistent face-to-face encounter which may be too intense:

> Well there was this one time I was talking to my friend in New York about something that happened regarding another friend in Trinidad. So it was kinda like a dispute you would say. So I was kinda angry and upset and well she was trying to talk me through it. Like you know, saying that it wasn't my fault or the other friend's fault either. I don't know, she was sort of moderating I guess. So in that case I was upset. So that's the time when I was staring off into space and I wasn't looking at her because I just, I couldn't look at her to say, you know, I don't know, to deal with it I guess. The problem for her was partly that she could imagine putting down the phone at that moment because it was getting difficult for her to control her anger and other feelings, but she didn't feel she could do that with Skype because I guess, seeing as we make the time and effort to sit down, so you don't want to throw it away and be like 'bye, I have something else to do' because you already allotted that time for them already, so you don't really have anything else to do otherwise you wouldn't be Skyping right.

Once again, the problem is how to take power and control not to gain authority, but in order not to offend the other person, to respect what they are trying to do for you. Because webcam is found to have such a strong emotional aspect, this becomes that much harder to achieve. To take a final example – a man talking about his long-distance relationship:

> With family here, you could be yourself and you could afford to get as angry as you like and tomorrow is another day. You will see them. But dealing with her, I'm conscious that I don't really want to upset her because tomorrow I won't see her and I won't be able to fix it. I will get to Skype her by the weekend. So you're not as open as you would like to be because you have to be guarded, because she just so far away.

As in several of the previous examples, we see here the contradictions of Skype. This stems from the feeling that to webcam someone, unlike merely meeting them in the street, is a special investment of attention, but this limits the way you can use it. You can't afford the openness because you don't have the immediate chance to resolve any issues that thereby arise. The relevance of this to the discussion of polymedia is that in all these conversations, people are alluding to alternative ways to communicate, whether by phone or by email, to help resolve the contradictions that are experienced in webcam. It is by no means just academics who argue that social relationships are also power relationships. Our informants would recognize this whether talking about parenting, sibling rivalries or formation of couples. It is often in those charged emotional encounters and outbursts when power is revealed as a facet of relationships. But it is precisely because people recognize this that they seek to engage with power as something that could either weaken or strengthen that relationship. In developing long-term relationships of love and care, we seek to accentuate the positive qualities while ameliorating the concomitant negative aspects of most relationships, such as jealousy, competition or differential power. In short, polymedia is something that most people soon come to appreciate as a factor that can help them determine the way power and emotions operate within any given relationship. This is perhaps most clearly seen when we examine a relationship in its formation, as in the case of Olivia.

Olivia: Creating Relationships

Olivia also returns us to the earliest point of this chapter, which is that even when seen historically, our explanations are rarely reduced to the given propensities or affordances of a medium. It is as much the happenstance of how one follows from another that seems causative of the final configuration. There is so much serendipity to the way each medium comes to its position in these relationships.

Olivia is a curious case because in some ways her experience of webcam was diametrically opposed to that of the majority of the people we worked with. Olivia started experimenting with new media as a teenager. And what attracted her above all was the anonymity provided by those media. With devices such as ICQ, which feature prominently in Miller and Slater (2000), she loved the way she could play around with different personas, which meant that she could freely tell strangers all the problems she was having with her teachers and parents under the protection of anonymity. She also had pretend characters; in particular, one in which she herself had a daughter. She would link these to random photographs that she found online.

From this, she naturally progressed to platforms such as MSN to which she became very adept, and messaging and texting were her forté. These then became the proper, the authentic way of getting to know people. When the person, who later became her husband, first arrived in Trinidad as a trainee medic, visiting from the UK, although they saw each other almost every day for over two months, they barely got to know each other at all from face-to-face encounters. But they did become Facebook friends, and it was on that site that they both started to consider whether the other might be a rather more interesting person than they had realized. This was not, however, a suitable site for direct interaction. Olivia's problem was that Peter was not particularly into MSN or Yahoo messenger or, later on, BBM. This mattered because there was a very particular sequence of communication that she imagined as the proper way for her relationship to develop. She saw polymedia more in terms of a sequence of growing commitment, very different from the kind of simultaneous multi-tasking of Christian. It therefore became essential for her to persuade him into each of these media in succession. The other advantage of this was that she was always the more accomplished and skilled practitioner, always the teacher, rather than the pupil. He was coming to their relationship on her media turf. Over the year and a half between his first and his second visit, this strategy proved sufficiently successful. Their long-distance relationship had become increasingly personal and able to replace the relationships they each had had with other people.

Gradually but surely, they became convinced that they had fallen in love. They didn't really use webcam until the summer of 2009. At that time, Olivia didn't have a computer with webcam, so webcam became associated with some quite cumbersome scheduling of online meetings and frustration with time differences. Her lack of familiarity with this medium compared to those she had already mastered, and the need to plan these encounters, meant that the whole thing had an aura of formality and artificiality, especially as, at first, it was also asymmetrical as she could see him but he couldn't see her. She also didn't like the fact that she had to sit in one place for these sessions. The conversations seemed awkward. Being face to face, it was like you had to keep talking, you had to be prepared with the next question. She felt as though she was on camera and exposed. She wanted to hide behind the screen. It was all too pressured. Olivia would get self-conscious and just stare at herself in the corner, thinking about what angle made her face look best.

They tried to get around this. At one point they scheduled a Skype date during which they would watch a movie together (but in their separate locations). They thought that perhaps things would be easier when you don't have to talk to each other all the time. But that still didn't really work. Even the 'always-on' mode of webcam has only started to feel a bit more comfortable since they were married.

In fact, Skype nearly destroyed this relationship, because when they finally agreed that he should return and live with her for a month, she found herself extremely anxious. In her mind, the question was whether sex with Peter would be like Skype, rather cold and awkward and embarrassing. Or whether it would be like messaging, that is fun, informal and enjoyable. The very first couple of days were in fact a bit awkward, but soon things settled down, which was important since they both knew that the physical side of things needed to sort of catch up with the way everything else had by then developed. Fortunately, it did and they became an established couple who would later get married. Today, Skype still feels awkward, especially at the beginning of each session. And it will probably never seem natural, though it has a clear place in a relationship which was destined for another year of transnational separation despite their marriage, because of their respective training commitments (by the end of our study, this year was over and she migrated to join him in England). She still sees Skype as something that forces them to watch each other in an artificial manner. She calls the Skype conversation 'compressed', while she feels she can be more expansive through texting.

By way of contrast, during the same period that they were trying to work with Skype, Olivia managed to persuade Peter to buy a BlackBerry, much less familiar in the UK, and this became far more comfortable and successful as a medium between them. It didn't require any simultaneity of presence and seemed far more natural to Olivia. In fact, she now sees the BlackBerry as the device that made the relationship a success. In this case, the medium also came into its own once they were married. This is the device where she feels comfortable, taking up a more explicit and erotic mode of texting, what she, like many, calls sexting. This is clearly not because of any embarrassment about being visual. Olivia is extremely good looking by any standard, and aware of this. It is simply that texting carries for her an intimacy that webcamming will never possess. We cannot say how far it also matters that texting is the medium where she is clearly the more experienced and powerful.

In the transition between the discussion of Christian and that of BlackBerry, we noted that polymedia is both a configuration that can become the portrait of an individual and an issue of cultural normativity, as where the BlackBerry becomes quintessentially Trinidadian. Both of these factors are present in the example of Olivia. Peter, the Englishman, is probably a little bemused that the erotic is conveyed largely through a BlackBerry, which in England is more associated with business. BlackBerry has become part of his adaptation to Trinidad. Yet, the relationship of Olivia to webcam is anything but typical of Trinidad. It contrasts with almost everything we have written in this book. It is rather the happenstance of how it came to be the very opposite of the anonymity and invisibility that she had carefully crafted for herself out of prior media, which in turn had consequences for her relationship with Peter. Fortunately, this relationship did not depend upon any one medium because the final skill employed in its development was actually polymedia – getting the right configuration between all these media and the issues of power that they alluded to in order to finally make the relationship work.

Polymedia within Skype

Olivia uses the BlackBerry for sexting, but sex is also a rather good analogy for understanding the final section of this chapter, which is the topic of polymedia as something that exists within Skype and not just between Skype and other platforms. This book is about webcam, but the experience of webcam is dominated by Skype, and Skype is curious because it facilitates the combined use of three different media, those of voice, sight and text. As we have noted in several of the other chapters, many people type messages while on Skype, often texting things that for one reason or another they don't want to say out loud or have others see.

As anyone who reads women's magazines with any regularity will attest, good sex relies on paying attention to several of the senses and several parts of the body at once, which is not just a question of being dextrous in simultaneity but in understanding how the rhythm of one sense or erotic zone interacts with the others. It follows that a platform that allows for a subtle interplay between voice, sights and text also lends itself to this skill in intimacy. Sometimes, this relates to sex itself. For example, the man who admitted that he has never been able to talk much during sex, somewhat to the frustration of his partner, found that he took easily to texting during cybersex. It became a very suitable mode for telling his partner what he wanted her to do on screen, or for other forms of flirtatiousness that were quite effective as part of the overall erotic register that cybersex demands. Texting may have migrated to sexting for at least two other reasons. One is that, as with Olivia, there is already a tradition of erotic exchange associated with the BlackBerry and BBM; secondly, because often people talk of using text in intimate conversation on Skype as they are worried about being overheard, for example when Skyping from within the family home. In this case, texting takes on the task of communicating precisely the things you wouldn't want your parents to overhear. But good sex demands mutuality, and an older man complained about this with regard to trying to have cybersex with younger women. For him, this interplay of media should work through the subtleties of foreplay. He feels it is right to go through a sequence of increasingly revealing media prior to the explosion of sight. So actually, he is rather offended when the first thing a young woman does is go on Skype and whip off her blouse to expose herself.

Although not, strictly speaking, internal polymedia, one can also see other media being incorporated within Skype; for example, one girl uses the webcam to make videos to send to her boyfriend:

> Yes. We will use photos, I will email photos and stuff and we will chat, sometimes we would send videos. I hold it in my hand. Mix of close up and far away . . . I will take it like 7 times before I get a perfect one and I will choose one out of the 7 and send that one. The last one I sent was 7 minutes long. It does take really long to make it. Like 2 hours. We try to send a video once a week. I send it straight from my phone as an attachment. Yeah. Cos we make it at the same time. When I'm making it, I make sure he's making his at the same time, then I'm like 'you ready? Yuh gonna send me yours?' So I'll always send mine first and he will send his straight after. So we're making it at the same time. It helps a lot. I wouldn't do it for anybody else, I take the time to do it for him. Yes, I think it's the relationship and the connection that we do it for each other. Mine's more about the relationship [than sex].

Their use of Skype then builds from this, because Skype is interactive while the video is a more thoughtful constructed sequence sent as a gift to each other.

The points made about polymedia with regard to sex apply to other uses. There are many situations where texting is valuable; for example, a woman who is trying to get her nephew to behave, is talking to him over Skype, while simultaneously texting to her sister about she doesn't want the nephew to hear. The polymedia aspect of Skype is also important simply because of the technical unreliability of the media. It is extremely common to start Skype with simultaneous webcam and then discover that Skype freezes and they lose aspects of voice or the visual. For some, it's an expectation of almost every Skype call. So, having once reminded each other of how they look and checked that they are well, they mutually agree to remove the video element and carry on talking. If the connection is even worse and the voice is unreliable, then they resort to texting only. The problem is that if people don't exploit the polymedia within Skype, they may end up just fixating on the failings of the technology to the detriment of the relationship: 'Oh yeah, for him, he gets really hysterical. He gets so angry, it's really quite funny. Like I'm pretty chilled out, but he goes berserk. Like "I CAN'T HEAR YOU!!!" . . . So he would get sooo soo pissed off and angry.'

One potential for polymedia within Skype, which was used rather less than we had predicted, was the facility within most modern webcams to take screenshots. A few people talked of doing this and then finding the one in which the person looked at their worst or most comic in order to post these on Facebook. This worked well with a group of international school friends, helping them to bond as a group. We have mentioned the sex/porn site specific to Trinidad, where people post explicit pictures of their girlfriends, most likely taken without their knowledge, which may sometimes be the result of their abuse of this facility, though we have no evidence for this. Another form of polymedia is when people have several screens, one of which concentrates on always-on webcam, while the other screen can be used for different media or activities.

Finally, there is just one more quality of Skype that we have barely mentioned, yet seems entirely appropriate to the fading out of this chapter on polymedia. It is that small red or green dot that does nothing more than indicate whether another person is presently at their own computer and potentially available for webcam. Often, this is of little significance, but sometimes it turns out to be hugely important, especially for people who are feeling insecure or lonely. A daughter living abroad for the first time wants to know that her mother is 'present', even in that absolutely minimal sense of a potential if-and-when. Similarly, a girl uncertain of her relationship with her boyfriend is reassured by a symbol that tells her he is 'there for her' but without her having to actually disturb or intrude upon his time. These dots could be regarded as a kind of minimal unit of sociality. Some couples like it to be there only for each other, so that they have a kind of very low level always-on aspect to webcam use. Others prefer to put themselves as absent on Skype simply because otherwise it leads to intrusive calls. In Chapter Two, we presented Colin manipulating this facility as part of a quarrel. So, these dots seem to have occupied a niche as a minimal form of always-on reassurance for people wanting to have at least some sense of the simultaneous presence of the other.

All of this implies that one of the reasons for the success of Skype is that it is much more than just webcam. It includes other media such as voice and text, as well as this almost unnoticed aspect of potential presence. These multiple facilities of Skype make this an excellent illustration of polymedia, where the meaning of any one medium must always be understood in relation to all the other choices available. When we discussed the theory of attainment in Chapter One, the references were mainly to technological changes and the way we appropriate new technology as an integral part of what we do and thereby who we are. There is a danger that this becomes simplified to the appropriation of each singular technology in turn, a problem we may have contributed to by virtue of having a book called 'webcam'.

This chapter has therefore an essential role in trying to balance the conclusion drawn from this research. People never experience a communication technology in isolation, and, increasingly, what technological change affects is not a single new facility but the experience of selection. The reason polymedia as a theory works so well with a theory of attainment is that, from the beginning, we have argued that polymedia is not merely about a proliferation of different technologies. Our emphasis has been on the way this re-socializes communication as a moral issue in that we are now judged as to which media or which combination of media we employ. Attainment is about recognizing the way media works internally as part of the infrastructure of who we are. Unlike other theories, we don't start with a given, the person or the population who then uses something external called a technology. Our theory of attainment states that technology changes who we are not because we are becoming, as most people suggest, more technological, or more mediated. It is because we always existed with a tangible skeletal infrastructure and a less tangible technological infrastructure, which includes the form and nature of communication as part of our cultural make-up. Understanding webcam as polymedia reinforces the idea that using it is always a social and moral issue, which is why we paid particular attention to dimensions such as power and emotion. Polymedia contributes to our theory of attainment, because it is an argument that the normative nature of communication is made more evident by the condition of choice.

7

Visibility

Webcam as truth and trust

The previous chapters have introduced a range of topics that emerged from our ethnographic study of webcam usage. Yet, up to now, we have avoided what most people might have anticipated would be the central topic for any discussion of webcam, whatever the context of its use. This is the consequences of visibility itself. Is this a rather more fundamental property of webcam which needs to be abstracted and considered in its own right? Instead of entirely embedding webcam usage within social relationships, couldn't we just for once allow this essential feature to be a focus of attention and consideration in its own right? This chapter is intended to answer these questions and to ensure that visibility is allowed to rise from being merely a premise to other discussions, to take its proper place as the core facility that webcam brings to communication and that we clearly need to appreciate in order to understand the consequences of webcam.

In some ways, this should be a more straightforward exercise than ethnographic analysis, as there is a long history of trying to understand the abstracted properties of new media as they arose. An account of such studies may be found in the first half of chapter three in Baym's book *Personal Connections in the Digital Age* (2010: 51–7). She looks back at earlier theorizing of media, as it emerged from more commercial settings, where people were trying to establish some measure of the gains brought by each new medium. There seemed a natural tendency to rank media, with those such as face to face that offer the most cues coming at the top, while the more mediated go to the bottom. With these commercial ends in view, academics tried to determine the efficacy and pitfalls of various media. The two main approaches were 'Social Presence Theory', that is our sense of the degree to which we feel the other person is present, examining, for example, the importance of non-verbal cues. Secondly, there was 'Media Rich Theory', which focused more on the capacity of certain media to convey information. Later on, other approaches, such as social constructionism, were added to this mix (Fulk, 1993). Baym argues that such research tended to produce misleading conclusions, because the methods were based on artificial experiments, while a more contextualized approach helps us to appreciate that the issue is less what technology does to us and more what we find we are able to do with technology, which leads us back to a consideration of context.

With this caveat in mind, we will take our cue from Baym, in that we will focus on commercial usage. The previous chapters of this book emphasize relationships, but webcam is involved in many other forms of communication, especially in the field of commerce. On the other hand, unlike the theorists discussed by Baym, we will not refer to decontextualized experiments, but to the way webcam has become part of everyday communication within business contexts. As the chapter develops, we will see that any simple opposition of personal relationships to commercial usage is in any case quite false, since an examination of webcam within business proves quite trenchant in helping further our understanding of what is at stake in the use of webcam within relationships. This turn to commerce has another advantage in that it helps to remind us that webcam comes with a prior history, which is likely to have repercussions upon its current meanings, and which also directs our attention to the current issue of visibility. Within the trajectory of commercial usage, there were two employments of webcam that dominated prior to the invention of Skype. The first was the use of webcam as CCTV (Norris and Armstrong, 1999), which exploited visibility as a form of surveillance. The other was the use of webcam within pornography and, specifically, the genre of 'camgirls' (Senft, 2008), which again exploited webcam's potential to create visibility for commercial purposes. These two precedents have only played a minor role in previous chapters, but come to the fore when we consider visibility per se.

Immediately, on considering the use of webcam for businesses, we find a blurring of boundaries between webcams attached to computers and used for Skype, and webcam as it has evolved into the world of CCTV and security cameras, for which the key property is not communication but recording and bearing witness to the truth of events. We are increasingly familiar with webcam as evidence in legal cases. It is common for a news broadcast to now show rather indistinct images of the victim or perpetrator on CCTV as part of their coverage of the crime. Such cases build upon a long history of new media being seen as a potential for new forms of surveillance, by virtue of their capacity to create new forms of evidence (Lauer, 2011).

A shopkeeper talked of changing his business model to develop ordinary computer webcams into CCTV for farmers in the region who were concerned with their crops and property. Although this was just in his imagination, he could envisage the increased use of webcam as a security device on analogy with the ideal of 'an internet of things' (Ashton, 2009), where surveillance could make use of the multiplicity of webcams. As he put it, 'Because every device now has a webcam, your phone has a webcam sometimes, your iPad has a webcam, laptops have built-in webcams, anywhere you turn, you see a webcam.' For him, this was a benign potential, rather than the malign Big Brother consequence of surveillance. Another informant who used CCTV for business had extended his contract to the security firm and now has 24-hour surveillance of his own property as part of the package.

Perhaps the most popular, but also controversial programme on Trinidad television at the time of our fieldwork was called *Crime Watch*. The programme is almost entirely dependent on rebroadcasting film of people being caught on CCTV. But it thereby also exposed many of the issues in using such material. At one point, the programme was taken off the air, and the presenter Ian Alleyne arrested because it was alleged that he had broadcast the rape of an identifiable teenage girl (*Trinidad Guardian*, 21 April 2012).

This alerts us to a critical contradiction in the qualities of visibility. Visibility as attested reality is matched by concerns over the proper limits to visibility as impinging upon privacy. In *Crime Watch*, webcam becomes hero when it leads to the conviction of the rapist, but villain when broadcasting the victim of a rape on television. The implied voyeurism incorporates our second precedent, and another familiar contradiction, in which webcam as attested reality is contrasted with webcam as a facilitator of fantasy because of its use within pornography. Camgirl fantasy seems at first a far cry from this legalistic usage of webcam as court evidence. Yet, on reflection, what they share is an imagination of veracity and authenticity. The whole point in pornography is that this is taken to be a real person you are watching masturbate through the screen. Given these connotations of both veracity and authenticity, it is not surprising that when we come to enquire into the role of visibility in communication, we are soon mired in these muddier issues of trust, evidence and fantasy.

The point is that visibility implicates a sense of truth beyond that of other evidence such as the aural. One of the most influential discussions of this quality of the visual was Roland Barthes' 1977 essay 'Rhetoric of the Image', which brought out many of the most pertinent issues. Employing the term 'rhetoric' in the title foregrounds his core argument, which is that visibility is itself a performative action based on the resonance of truth itself. By using as his example an advertisement, he demonstrates that this is a performance of truth, not actual veracity. Barthes analyses an advertisement for Italian pasta and the way it played with the colours of the Italian flag, and with the inclusion of fresh ingredients to create an aura around the pasta of both freshness and authentic Italianicity. At a meta-level, the mere fact that it used a photograph, rather than say a drawing, implied a certain ideal of truthfulness that seems to attest to such claims. Yet as an advertisement, this is entirely an artifice.

All the points raised by Barthes with regard to the photograph as still image seem to be accentuated in the case of webcam. Its proximity to CCTV, its apparently greater evidential impact, compared to the mere photo as sustained live image, makes that rhetoric of veracity that much stronger. Yet, at the same time, it is just as susceptible to rhetoric. Once we balance the CCTV with pornographic webcam fantasy, we can see that even in the news broadcast, it is the performance of truth that is central. Within pornography, the end of the performance is often extreme close-up shots of male (or female) ejaculation, partly because this attests to actual rather than faked orgasm (Fernandes, 1991; Monroe, 2010). This suggests that webcam, just as much as the still photo, seems to bring with it the suspicion of artifice even as it adds to the claims for truth.

So while it may sound pretentious, there are genuine grounds for seeing webcam as a dialectical shift. The term dialectical is used here to suggest something that simultaneously extends both opposing polarities of an argument. Compared to the photograph or the phone, webcam seems both more truthful, pushing the possibilities of evidence, and at the same time more false, extending the potential for faking, which makes the tension between truth and its opposite that much more exquisite. This is what leaves audiences in thrall, not just to pornography, but to an equally widespread voyeurism of crime fiction and crime fact as when watching a programme such as *Crime Watch*. But equally, this becomes integral to the routine watching of news, where we are drawn into making our own judgements as to the evidential properties of what we see on the screen. These are the programmes, news, crime and eroticism, that dominate much of popular television, suggesting that we are dealing with something of considerable contemporary significance.

As in the analysis by Barthes, we start to appreciate that webcam brings with it a kind of meta-level of truth awareness in that we cannot lose our knowledge of the presence of webcam itself, or regain the innocence of a pre-webcam existence. As it becomes more ubiquitous, it also can become presumed, and therefore we become anxious at the absence of the visual. Now, the mere refusal to have webcam makes us suspicious and lacking. Perhaps the most eloquent rendition of this anxiety came from someone not in the commercial sector, but just describing an issue that has arisen in talking to a friend. He states:

> Personally, I cannot talk to someone without seeing their face, my friend in New Orleans, she doesn't like to talk without the webcam so she would be talking to you and then she'd be like 'can you please put on your webcam' and I'll be like 'arite yeah, no problem' because I don't like to do it [talk without webcam], but my other friend, she does be talking to other people while she's speaking to me so she doesn't want to put on the camera sometimes, so she

> would put on the Skype call and talk and then I'll be like 'put on your camera, because I can't talk to you, I'd rather IM you than talk to you.'

Although he knows the reason may just be that a woman doesn't want to be seen without having finished her makeup, he can't suppress a feeling of anger that stands for his presumption that if a truth is now embodied in the very existence and possibility of webcam, then it becomes wrong, a falsehood, a sin, to be talking on Skype without the webcam actually on. One way in which this chapter follows directly upon the last was that polymedia was seen to not just re-socialize but also re-moralize media choice. To refuse webcam and neglect that capacity to be seen can become a judgement upon you, imputing the motives behind this preference. All of these points become still clearer when we turn to the topic of webcam in commercial usage, where we see that webcam has become intimately associated with issues of trust, both trust in the technology as truth but equally as trust in other people.

Prakash is a middle-aged Trini who lives alone on the outskirts of Arima and works from home, where he has converted his front yard and garage into a small mechanic's shop. Prakash's largest annoyance is that he often gets customers asking him for the cheapest service without paying attention to the high quality of the service that he feels he delivers. Conversely, when he buys parts, he is often wary that suppliers, often small businesses like himself, will sell him inferior parts at a higher cost.

> Because everybody twists things, especially Trinidadians. I don't do that because that means you're doing shortcuts, you're buying cheaper stuff, cutting on fittings to make the customer happy. In Trinidad, people don't appreciate a better mechanic, they appreciate a cheaper job, they will come and fix the same cheap part ten times rather than buying one good part. But some parts-supplies store, they have a Skype account, things like that I would use it. Like if the guy says to Skype him, I'd prefer to talk to someone in person than to send an email. Maybe I can see where they are working. I don't think I'd get to see their warehouse and so on, but at least I'll get to talk to somebody, rather than sending a blank email to somebody you don't know. If you have a little bit of experience in life, you could read somebody's face to know if they're

> truthful to you or if they're messing around because I know there are a lot of con artists all over.

Similarly, Jeren works in customer service for a furniture company. Clients mostly place orders with him via email, but he will often use Skype to confirm details and show them products. 'That's a huge advantage with Skype over a telephone call and talking to customers, you can see their facial expressions, their reactions, sometimes if I say something and they don't agree with it, they will not say anything, but their facial expression does say a lot.' Sometimes, he will have to deal with client dissatisfaction on a video call, and when he does, he tries to be much more careful of his facial expression, not appearing defensive and remaining as neutral as possible, especially since the person doesn't know him very well.

The very possibility of Skype communication, now that it is so simple and possible to show oneself online, may make someone who seems unwilling to expose themselves in this way thereby appear shady or untrustworthy, even though most people also recognize that this sense of veracity is largely false. The fact that someone is willing to appear on camera in China does not in fact add one iota to the evidence that their commercial deal will be honoured or the quality of the product will be higher. Yet, this knowledge does not prevent a kind of inexorable drift towards the insistent and apparent truth content of visual presence as an integral aspect of trust. This also leads to an increasing awareness of cultural differences as to whether people feel it's appropriate to show themselves or not. As we shall see below, Trinidadians prefer to present themselves with a photo as a sign of their honesty rather than as a cartoon, which is common with correspondents in the US.

Similar issues arose in one of the arenas of increasing webcam use within commerce, which is for interviewing people living abroad. For example, when a Trinidadian firm is recruiting doctors and nurses from India, they look to see if the interviewee appears to be able to discuss things directly or whether they looking down at a piece of paper. Do you thereby gain a better sense, maybe not of how effective they are, but at least of how pleasant a person they will be to work with? A UK company that recruits nurses from abroad stopped sending teams to places such as Jordan and the Philippines and replaced this with web interviews, which they saw as far more reliable than phone interviews. They recognized that they would then need to take into account cultural sensitivities, such as that nurses from the Middle East clearly do not feel comfortable looking face to face but stared down at their shoes to demonstrate appropriate modesty, while, by contrast, it took a while to realize that nurses from Nigeria were not peculiarly aggressive just because they were far bolder in the way they looked at you while being interviewed.

As in social relationships, commercial usage soon brings out wider issues of ambivalence and contradiction. For example, a senior manager in a large firm has increasing problems as a result of the turn to webcam, which in her case she regards as taking us further away from guarantors of truth and trust. She is concerned with the way webcam is replacing email, which is a written document that constitutes a recording. Email can be stored and then used in evidence. By contrast, webcam is a transient, unrecorded medium that leaves no trace and is entirely open to dispute as to who promised what to whom. Perhaps surprisingly, we found no case of Skype being recorded in Trinidad (though this is very demanding of storage capacity), which has strong connotations of betrayal since the main instances that most people know of are those in which someone having cybersex was recorded without their permission or awareness that this was taking place. Only in the UK study did we encounter a woman who was recording her Skype conversations with her ex-partner without his knowledge with the aim of using these to improve her divorce settlement. So, ironically, the very medium that has now inveigled itself into our consciousness as an embodiment of truth is actually making it far more difficult to obtain useful evidence that can attest to commercial veracity. Indeed, many people now turn to webcam and Skype in commercial communication, precisely because it allows the informality of negotiation without a feeling that one is bound by what is said, exploiting the fact that this leaves no evidence. We started with webcam as evidence and we end here with the opposite. All of which reinforces our contention that webcam is best seen as a dialectical moment which simultaneously extends our capacity for and consciousness of the world as truth and as falsehood. Mostly this is not discussed directly, but has to be extracted from a discourse which is generally dominated by claims of functionality and efficiency.

Webcam as functionality and efficiency

The issue of security as a basic functionality has certainly been one route towards webcam's adoption in Trinidadian commerce. It is now as ubiquitous as the security guard in the protection of firms. A Trinidadian transnational company with 500 employees has even started using special webcam software for facial recognition as part of its security. For most companies, the integration of webcam as the product of functionality and efficiency is couched almost entirely in terms of cost. Will the use of webcam be cheaper than the alternative of phone? Does it mean that one can cut down on other expenses, most notably of travel?

Yet, a moment's reflection shows why this apparently tight economic logic of cost effectiveness and efficiency is actually in some ways rather bizarre. The first thing most companies will say is that they are moving to Skype because it is free, while the phone is not. It may also be the case that Skype adds the visual to the audio, but from a cost–benefit perspective that is seen as secondary. As we have noted on several occasions, why on earth should communication in which you can see as well as speak be cheaper than when you can only speak? The reason lies entirely within the fortuitous political economy of contemporary communication, in which voice communication by phone was introduced through commercial companies, often at high costs, while webcam developed as an add-on to an internet service that was associated with various models of open access and therefore cannot charge for the service. There is absolutely no logic to this except the happenstance of the historical development of these media. By rights, webcam with the visual should cost far more than mere speaking. This was the *natural* trajectory as understood by most telecommunication firms, who for years tried to persuade consumers to add videophone to their phone package, often at a rather considerable additional cost. But consumers leapfrogged the IT companies on the broad back of the internet. So this apparent cost efficiency is simply mass opportunism taking advantage of the vagaries and illogicality of the political economy of mass communication. In a similar fashion, the Philippines is the world's most prolific user of text because originally text was a free add-on to the phone, and the commercial companies that developed it had absolutely no idea how much people would come to use text (Pertierra et al., 2002).

None of which gainsays the potential cost/benefits of webcam as being of considerable interest to big business. In his book on capitalism in Trinidad, Miller (1997) noted that, if anything, Trinidad was an exporter rather than an importer of transnational corporations, which meant it was a good place to see the impact webcam can have on large companies. The Trinidadian transnational company mentioned above with 500 employees had recently installed at its headquarters a large screen with dedicated videoconferencing hardware. This cost US$15k, but was justified if it could save merely two trips by the company chair, who otherwise needs to visit Barbados, Jamaica, Miami and Guyana, typically over five days. And this was just the initial idea. After a while, they realized it was just as useful for communication within Trinidad, because there are many places that are a mere 20 minutes away from the capital when traffic is low, but which can be two or even three hours away during the morning and afternoon rush hours. Quite often, four or five of the 12 board members will be using the equipment, and the IT officers love the opportunities it gives them to fix problems across the company with much less travel. Another home-grown Trinidadian corporation described how webcam helps them maintain communication with the 60 companies they own worldwide, mainly in the Caribbean, Latin America and Florida, the main areas typically colonized by Trinidadian transnationals.

If webcam can create efficiencies in large businesses, it can also create viability in small ones. When Horst and Miller (2006) were studying the impact of mobile phones in Jamaica, a key expectation was that this would create a massive increase in small-scale businesses, as people no longer needed a fixed office and other assets, once they had mobile communication. They could simply trade by phone, although this turned out to be relatively rare. Webcam is unlikely to be quite so revolutionary in its potential, but for certain kinds of business venture it was possible to imagine things that would not previously have been viable. For example, one man in El Mirador wanted to develop a business in agrichemical products. But this would only work if the farmers living in a wide area around the town could use webcam to directly consult about plant disease and other matters, showing plants and animals in their natural settings and without the expense of coming to town to discuss these. Another was hoping that the huge popularity of *Crime Watch* would allow him to develop a business around home surveillance.

Webcam also makes possible new forms of transnational labour akin to 'body shopping' (Xiang, 2007). Body shopping involved bringing low paid computer experts from places such as India to countries such as the US or UK. By contrast, a Trinidadian who works transnationally now outsources his more monotonous tasks to a woman in the Philippines, while he concentrates on gaining and maintaining clients. He found her by interviewing through webcam, he has much of his correspondence with her by webcam and pays her through PayPal. 'She does good work. She works for eight hours a day, a forty hour working week for US$250 a month.' They also use webcam regularly with their clients, both to establish trust and to communicate, and they share the same concern to look appropriate, which fortunately in the IT sector is a fairly informal style.

Not surprisingly, it was within the IT sector that practitioners particularly enthused about having these visual connections to facilitate their work. As one IT expert put it, 'they retain 15 per cent of what they hear but about 75 per cent of what they see, so the webcam thingy, communicating through the webcam, really boost the relationship that we had with our people, who couldn't meet with me face to face'. Along with the better customer service, he felt it had given him his competitive advantage and explained much of his current success as a company.

A major arena of commercial usage is in training and education. It became clear quite early on that it is far more effective to teach someone a task when the teacher is visible and can use videos rather than relying on static diagrams and photographs. This runs in tandem to the non-commercial world, where there has been a huge growth in the advent of the YouTube guru. An excellent MSc essay in Digital Anthropology by Juliano Spyer (2011) at UCL looked at the growth of cosmetic gurus. These are young women, often around 16 years of age, who gain international reputations by showing other young women how to put on their makeup. In our fieldwork, people commonly talked of using webcam to learn dance and music, such as how to play guitar, where the advantages are both obvious and huge. Webcam has also become a routine part of school and college work. In Trinidad, this includes teachers discussing material with pupils at home, something that seems more possible and informal than might be the case in the UK. But in many countries, students now share school work and collaborate in their homework through webcam. Webcam is now also routine for transnational university degrees. Several people we met in Trinidad are currently taking courses in UK universities as external students, including occasional Skype supervisions with their tutors in the UK.

For example, one firm we interviewed had a business teaching a particular kind of martial arts to security workers using a technique developed in Israel. This posed some problems of security itself since the people selling this product didn't want their pupils to copy and then give away these instructions for nothing. The company talked in detail about how they could use webcam to film the action in real time and then repeat the moves slowly, indicating the various component parts that made this form of fighting effective.

This usage for instruction is not restricted to firms that regard themselves as teaching something. It has become equally important in the ordinary transactions of trade. Many firms now illustrate their products, where these are industrial processes, though a pre-prepared YouTube video. These can also be used to show samples or details. We also found that their customers often wanted a more personal guided tour for the buyer, so they could ask questions as they were being shown the process. One point made several times was that having a visual component, including gestures, helped when the communication was in a sort of pidgin English with problems of both accent and vocabulary, but where pointing and gesturing could help prevent misunderstandings. Generally, companies feel they are getting a better idea of what it is they are buying before they commit. Similarly, when it comes to issues with defects, repairs and other problems, it helps to be able to show these and to discuss them in person online. To conclude, we would still affirm that much of this is performative; seeing someone is not of itself evidence for their trustworthiness. Webcam can just as well be considered a meta-message, whereby firms perform modernity in using the latest facilities for visualization and communication in order to impress each other. But we should also acknowledge that there are many ways in which webcam does indeed seem to produce cost effective, efficient and functional advances that are demonstrable and sustained for commercial activities.

Webcam as community and sociality

Even in the initial discussion of surveillance, truth turned out to be intimately linked to trust. This is presumably why people wish to see each other even if there is no real advantage in securing veracity. It was clear that the more the risk involved, the fact that money is passing hands, or that an IT assistant may ask for a password, all created an imperative to actually see the person if one could. As someone in a lighting firm argued, 'especially when we get close to sealing transactions I'd like to have some face-to-face conversation.' The point is not that seeing people makes anything more secure, but rather that increasing anxiety becomes in and of itself in imperative to add visual contact between people.

Seeing your trading partner in China adds merely the sight of that person. The consequences may be greater when used to see people from more familiar backgrounds. Webcam may reveal all sorts of contextual information that leads to the same broadening of communication as would also occur in face to face, as in asking where they purchased that fabulous skirt, and sometimes to questions about what time they get off work and would they like to meet for a drink.

Context may refer to time as well as appearance. A Trinidadian who had dealt anonymously all year with a commercial supplier might feel that at Christmas it would be appropriate to have a webcam conversation, which may take the correspondent in another country by surprise, if there is no such analogous expectation. This derives from long-held Christmas traditions in Trinidad (Miller, 1994: 92–3), where it was the custom that while people did not generally invite their work colleagues to their homes at any other time of the year, they did pay a personal visit around the Christmas season. Here, webcam would be a remediation of an older custom.

This, in turn, leads us to a hugely significant role of new media in demolishing the traditional firm barrier between work and the rest of life built up over the previous century and more. An extensive study by Broadbent (2011) in Switzerland shows an extraordinary and rapid transformation within capitalism. For a century and a half, business tried to insulate work into a cocoon so as to be freed from the distractions of family life and recreate workers as mechanical instruments within a process of production for profit. A mere two decades has been enough to demolish these fences. As computers became ubiquitous, and especially when email became the main form of business correspondence, people routinely added personal communication to work. The final barriers fell to the onslaught of smartphones, when Facebook and similar activities, forbidden on computers, could be accessed regardless. Parents, especially mothers, whose anxieties about their children have by no means diminished just because previously they were unable to communicate with them, are now able to stay in touch through the day, or at least feel they are on hand for emergencies. With webcam starting to migrate to smartphones, this will come to include visual contact.

A form of webcam communication that is starting to impinge upon some of our informants is the tricky issue of how one appears as available to Skype when the webcam is off. This is only now emerging because in commerce, as in relationships, the first model of the webcam is that of the videophone and only very recently as the technology improves are people beginning to realize the wider possibilities. 'Always-on' has not yet spread into work relations, except within the realm of surveillance, but with Skype there is the option of red dot unavailability and green dot availability. Being available could represent friendship and reassurance, but it could also result from the pressure of being available to one's boss at all times. Women are now confused as to whether they should maintain their 'work face' at home in case the boss Skypes them, and may subtly ensure that the webcam is poorly focused unless they are confident they have the appropriate appearance – in which case it can be finely focused.

In both the previous discussions, we imagine mainly a communication between two people, creating trust or friendship beyond work-based functionalism. But webcam can also be used for more than simple dyadic communication. We found hardly any instances of using Skype Premium, which allows for multiple presences, but companies may have invested in other more expensive forms of videoconferencing that are designed for groups. This is of considerable importance, given the number of both professional and commercial institutions that are dominated today by the ubiquitous committee meeting, or board meeting. In parallel to families presenting themselves as a whole to relatives abroad on occasions such as birthdays, there are many occasions for group participation in work which may also include celebrations as one branch of a company 'meets' another. As we go from the dyad to the group, we approach another overarching factor, which is the potential contribution of webcam to a more general ideal of community that transcends both efficiency and technology and sees sociality as a goal in its own right. This shift from community to communitas is developed through the following example of Madeira Shoes.

Madeira Shoes

For most companies, the initial potential of webcam is mostly a matter of cheap communications. But for Madeira Shoes, it touched on the foundations of its viability as a company. The individual who had founded, developed and still ran the company, had some years ago migrated to the US Midwest, which is where he saw the long-term future for his family, and which was where his wife originally came from. With nine children, this represents a commitment to more than just place, because he also wanted to invest more time in raising his children, and had decided that that meant creating more distance from his work, literally. One of the reasons he felt able to do this was precisely the improvements in communication between Trinidad and the US. Another of the company directors lives in Florida, while the remaining three live in Trinidad, which is where all the company operations are based. Although the owner left five years ago, when Skype was not sufficiently developed to have weighed in their considerations to the same extent as the phone, it has subsequently become integral to these arrangements. Today, as an executive noted, 'whenever there is a decision, something has to be discussed that's of strategic importance, be it investments of a substantial nature, a new strategy, anything of strategic importance, we call a committee meeting and we have the discussion over Skype.'

Given the still difficult functionality of Skype, this has as much to do with its usage as a conference call as to the visual, which can be easily lost when you try to have several people simultaneously online. On the other hand, the visual is immensely important. Skype contains a shared screen function, which is little known to people who are only interested in personal connections, but was widely referred to by those who use it for business functions. For them, a key feature was not being able to see faces, so much as everyone being able to focus on the same spreadsheet that they were all discussing. It was having a shared point of reference that makes many tasks viable. For such matters, location is irrelevant. It really didn't matter if one of those taking part was actually in Hong Kong sourcing materials, rather than in their office in Trinidad. It could, however, impact on other matters. In the past, holiday time was a genuine absence, but the company CEO noted that when he took his holiday this year in Scotland, it was a kind of qualified holiday, in that when something really important came up, he was still available to Skype. Also important to them was the green dot as opposed to a red one, which informed people that an individual could potentially be contacted. In general, short dyadic conversation tended to be phone based, while Skype conversations were seen to connote a more serious commitment, as they could last two hours and more.

All of these meant that new ambiguities arose in terms of appearance and presence. There were questions of whether one was 'dressed' for work and how self-conscious to be about having to actually appear online. One example evolved around the issue of *bareback* for men, which in Trinidad means simply a man not having anything on his top half:

> I might be home on the computer, laptop on my bed, bareback, and he would Skype me because he realize that he wants to say something to me and he realize that I am on the computer, and when the video comes on you realize wait nah, you know, you're bareback, and so you either put something on or take off the video . . . I suppose if I'm speaking with a female, I wouldn't want to be bareback, I know my boss very well, I would say that we are friends so I wouldn't be uncomfortable. My wife might be uncomfortable with me being bareback, so if she's in the room and she realize that I'm bareback and it's being shown, you know she may express some concern, but you know I wouldn't be uncomfortable with him.

The contrast was with another director he describes as 'prim and proper', who would never show himself as available on Skype other than in office hours and would never appear other than in suitable executive wear.

Appearance could also impinge in more subtle ways. A board member noted that you can't hold your head in disbelief at the stupidity of what the other has just said, or go off and find some water to drink in the middle of their long exposition, now that you can be seen. This shows how in some ways webcam turns out to be a return to deceit in business, as you thereby suppress the visual evidence of disagreement or disdain. A quintessentially Trinidadian way of discussing this was to make reference to the 'silent steups'. A steups is the characteristic way Trinis suck their teeth in annoyance, frustration or disdain. Normally, there is an accompanying sound, but on the phone one might do this action but silently, so the other person could not hear. Webcam ups the ante considerably in terms of self-monitoring how one appears to the other.

Apart from these issues of communication at the level of company directors, the other people to whom webcam is a huge issue were the IT officers. For one thing, they were responsible for making sure connections with the owner were properly maintained. They were a first port of call in troubleshooting the owner's computer facilities in the US. For this purpose, it was another of those less well-known properties of Skype that was critical, which is the ability to take over the other person's screen. Things had been vastly more difficult when the owner had to describe the problem over the phone, and the IT officer couldn't see it, let alone manipulate the computer from his own machine. Now things are much more straightforward.

The IT officers are also responsible for facilitating the connections between the owner and everyone else. And perhaps because the owner lived abroad, he was particularly demanding. Now that webcam was a possibility, he had high expectations to be able to see the person he was communicating with '99 per cent of the time'. The owner is convinced that being able to see someone's facial expressions gives him a better sense of what they are thinking: 'that's how he is, so I think it's more from his point of view he would like that because he's really distant from it, so those little fine points that he may miss, he would like that interactive ability.'

The IT officers also tend to reiterate the points about how Skype adds not just the visual, but a more personal, more holistic encounter with other people more generally. For example, working with contacts in the US it was suggested:

> Yeah, actually we've gotten to a point where, although it's a professional relationship, it's very cordial and very relaxed, because of Skype I would have to say. Yeah, before it was by telephone, you call and you create what is called a work ticket and they have it there for the programmer to pull and the programmer will call me back and say 'I see you have this issue, did you try so and so' and the whole idea is that it's over telephone, there's a cost, let's keep it short, let's get to the point. Whereas with Skype, he would respond, he would actually be doing some programming while I am there with him and I may ask 'how's the family?' or 'what's the weather like there?' And it developed from there to now I know how much kids he has, he knows how much kids I have. He asks a lot about Trinidad, and even makes jokes in between the work. So rather than just be silent and wait for a response, you're able now to talk to him and joke with him and not worry about the cost.
>
> Actually, let me give you an instance of the turn of a situation. The programmer I normally dealt with, the main programmer, our main rep, was at a remote site, he could not deal with me, he passed me on to another programmer that I knew, but I only knew him in passing, just phone. I told him I said, 'listen, do you wanna Skype this?' he said 'sure' so I sent an invitation and when he came in I had my picture. Now what I find is that Americans tend to have Charlie Brown or some animated picture, but Trinidadians tend to put a photo of themselves, because I think we deal more personally than they do, and he saw my picture and he said 'Aye I didn't know you were so old' and he said 'you got a lot of grey hair.' He say he always thought I was young and we chatted for about five minutes. And I built a relationship with him right there, in so far as I asked him 'do you want me to put through a work ticket for this? Is this gonna be a problem?' and he told me 'nah, don't worry, we could fix it right now quickly', you see, so that personal link there with Skype, has now created another connection for me that ensures that if I have an issue, I can get something done very quickly because of that personal relationship.

IT officers clearly have a more intimate relationship with the communication infrastructure itself. One of those we spoke with suggested that a reason he had left his previous work in a bank to come to work for Madeira Shoes is that he has far more freedom to envisage and push through new technologies. For example, he knows Madeira Shoes has a particularly good reputation for customer service, so he is imagining how Skype could be directly employed in the future within that sector. With his four laptops and two tablets at home, he has managed to cut his driving bill from 2k to 1k dollars this year, because he can do so much more from home. He can envisage many such improvements he would like to spread around the company. One of his tricks is to install Skype and then after a while remove it, since he has found that the more conservative elements in the company are much more inclined towards progress once it is a matter of them losing something rather than because he appears to be promoting something new.

Often, the technology itself acts as the push towards modernization. 'They wanna buy a laptop and so on and the first thing they ask with a laptop, "does it have a camera and microphone? Can I use Skype on it? Because a lot of people that are now buying laptops want to communicate with family in the US and Skype is free.' They are also upgrading their phones: 'You see Skype is something that is so important, what you see it does on a computer. To have to have something limited on your phone, you don't want that. You'd rather get something very close to what you're getting on your computer on your phone, which then means you'd have to upgrade your phone, so Skype is leading to that want to have the technology.' The pressures work in tandem: 'Any new employees, new managers and so on, we create a Skype account for them. It is now a directive from our owner that all managers have a Skype account so that he can communicate with them directly.'

None of this is terribly surprising. What we didn't anticipate, however, was the way that the wider ideal of sociality would manifest itself. It turned out that at Madeira:

> We have a core prayer group. They have prayer meetings using Skype. Because this company is a Christian based company, the owner is a Christian, a Pentecostal, he just prefers to say a Born-Again Christian. And he is in the US and the members of the board,

> primarily the directors, are Christian and they Skype and pray. About four separate parties at four different locations. And we have what is called an intercessor, someone who prays for the company and she is at another location and then you have two or three people at this location and they are all together on Skype . . . Well we had what was called a Proverbs meeting, it's not mandatory, managers, supervisors, administrators can come in at a particular time, on a particular day of every week for one hour and discuss a proverb. And you go through the whole proverb and discuss how it relates to the work environment and/or personal issues and what you think, and what can be contributed. The essential prayer group which is basically directors and the owner and they have moved to Skype because basically the owner has moved away.

Conclusions to this chapter

This would seem an odd chapter. With the title of visibility, one might have expected a narrow focus, trying to tease out exactly what we mean by the visual and how we experience it. The temptation is to assume that a chapter dedicated to visibility requires us to become more like natural scientists, digging down to issues of the cognitive. We would need to consider the universal or psychological attributes that are defining of the visual. We might have encountered the kinds of theorizing that Baym (2010) records from the earlier commercial attempts to determine and rank different media according to functionality and their ability to convey certain kinds of information.

The decision to concentrate on our evidence from usage by companies was intended precisely to both incorporate and to challenge the use of commercial criteria such as efficiency. We wanted to include issues such as functionality as part of visibility and to recognize that commercial usage opens up many important additional components to webcam that are less pertinent to the focus on personal relationships in other chapters. But at the same time, we have tried to make clear through the content of this chapter that such criteria are not in opposition to personal relationships, but, as with issues of trust, open up new avenues for considering the way personal relationships are integral to these same commercial considerations. In turn, this helps us appreciate how, for social science, the visual is not an abstract entity, or collection of properties. It is best constituted through the question of what is at stake in visibility.

In analysing our evidence, we forge this compromise between more abstract and more socially embedded factors by dividing our discussion into three main areas: the visual as a form of evidence or truth, the visual as an effective means to convey information, and the visual as the ability to see persons. In each case, this starts with something that sounds like a more abstract property of the visual as a medium, but soon transmutes into something closer to the beliefs that our informants have about such properties and the consequences this has for their relationships.

In the first case, the importance of the visual as evidence and truth seemed to arise out of the linkage between webcam as communication and two precedents – webcam as surveillance as in CCTV, and webcam as authenticity exemplified by camgirls. Soon we found that this pursuit of truth flows into issues of trust and character. Furthermore, the issue of veracity evoked Barthes' 1977 arguments regarding the meta-connotation of truth that seem inherent in the visible nature of photography, juxtaposed with the fact that the photograph Barthes analysed was being used for advertising. We show how webcam appears to accentuate all these contradictions previously found in the photograph, which led to the conclusion that webcam dialectically expands the conditions for what people take to be both truth and falsehood inherent in the property of visibility.

Similarly, companies see greater efficiency in the transference of information as webcam can display an industrial process or become more effective in training, as compared to the use of still images or voice alone. But then we also find that people are just as concerned to use webcam to merely see another person, such as their trading partner in China, which adds nothing to the information, but seems to reduce anxiety over an important transaction. In the case of Madeira Shoes, functional efficiency was found to be a motif within its aspirations to appear more up-to-date than its competitors. Furthermore, webcam as the technology of the visual was adopted just as much because of the happenstance of political economy, where bizarrely Skype also makes voice calling free. We don't want to exaggerate cultural relativism and deny the impact of efficiency and function. There is little reason to doubt that webcam is more effective in conveying an industrial process, or collectively examining a spreadsheet than a medium which lacks the capacity to show. It is rather that that effectiveness cannot be disaggregated from its wider connotations and cultural significance, which is often the reason it is of concern.

This explains our third category. Seeing people is not technically a different process from seeing things. It is not in itself a different form of visibility. But in practice, we found that whether the concern is surveillance or interactivity, the dominant theme was very often that persons were now visible. So what does it mean to 'see' another person? As in our chapter on intimacy, being within the cognitive sight of another person is nothing. Being seen is really an acknowledgement of the subject as a person and thereby the constitution of a relationship of some kind. It may be minimal, as in seeing the person from China one is transacting with, but usually it is far more than this. It seems highly appropriate to have ended our discussion with a scene where the staff of Madeira Shoes use Skype to pray together, because this brings out the highest values of sight, as expressed by theologians such as Buber (2000) and Levinas (Hand, 1989), an ethical aspiration for the acknowledgement of the other in their humanity, as constituted by God and within a context of communitas.

This may sound an overly pretentious way of approaching such a basic function as visibility. Yet it is consistent with the way Trinidadians viewed webcam. For them, it was always, or should always, be personal. The individual must be present, not as a Charlie Brown cartoon, but at least as a photograph. Surveillance as the truth of the person, efficiency as in the ability to know them better, trust that follows from both of these, are properties of the personal. So the technical ability to have something in the line of sight is commonly subservient to the social concern with how much of a person one is really seeing and acknowledging. As a result, while this chapter took a vicarious route through commercial usage, we have reinforced the arguments of other chapters, whose focus has been on personal relationships. Even the essential property of visibility in commerce may turn out to lie in those emotional and affective aspects of relationships that are deemed to be made available or facilitated by the presence of webcam.

A theory of attainment in the light of our ethnography

This book is a little unusual in that the conclusions that pertain to the volume as a whole are found in the first chapter. Our reason for switching things around was in order to be as open as possible as to the ambitions of this project and the kinds of claims we wanted to make. The intention was to expose the subsequent chapters to critical appraisal as to whether they seemed sufficient to substantiate those initial claims, rather than delivering theory as rabbits pulled out of our hats at the finale of our presentation. This narrative order also seemed to fit within our primary methodology, that which links ethnography to anthropology. Method consists of constantly juxtaposing the humanism present in the intimacy of ethnographic encounters against the analytical and theoretical arguments that they speak to.

The first chapter also made clear that we set sail in full consciousness of the perils of our journey. That we should keep clear of the Scylla represented by claims that webcam, as part of new digital media, was forging some new version of the post-human, or a world so removed from our pasts as to be no longer susceptible to understanding through the tools of academic scrutiny. We do not see webcam as harbinger of some techno-liberational utopia. Equally, we would not have wished to be trapped in the eddies of Charybdis, where we become lost in dreams of past authenticity, bemoaning the sad fate of our present to retain real or true forms of sociality.

Instead, this research was intended to demonstrate one of the core principals of an emerging digital anthropology (Horst and Miller, 2012), that this should not set out to be merely a treatise on how social science can help us to understand the use of webcam. It was always and equally intended as an exercise in showing how a study of webcam can help us to progress social science. What we find extraordinary about webcam is the way that again and again it has allowed us to reveal and appreciate prior forms of mediation. These were generally present, but relegated to the 'blindingly obvious', so evident that we have failed to really see them. A clear example came in Chapter Four. The best precedent for the arguments about co-presence had been the work of

Goffman, who revealed the careful construction of self-presentation for the purpose of public encounters. Much of this is unconscious and embedded in frames which ensure that we feel comforted by normative behaviour such as the proper form of greeting or proxemics and uncomfortable when we experience a failure to abide by these expectations. But Goffman's work pertained to various public domains where he could observe such interactions. It was only through the consideration of always-on webcam, when separated couples attempt to reconstruct the conditions of living together within the same house, that we came to appreciate how there could have been a whole other 'Goffman', revealing the extraordinary balance of communication and autonomy that allows two people to co-habit over the long term within the same space. While countless novelists exploit the exquisite tensions that result, social science has been slow to plough these rich fields of intimate privacy. Webcam helps us to appreciate what we have been missing.

In the introduction to the book *Digital Anthropology* (Miller and Horst, 2012), this approach is taken as foundational because it rests upon the anthropological premise that all human communication is equally mediated because it is equally cultural. Mediation does not grow or shrink. It is the intrinsic condition of being social. So we rejected the idea that webcam increases mediation, accepting only that it changes the nature of that mediation. In the conclusions to this book as presented in our first chapter, this point became the first leg that supported our development of a theory of attainment.

One of the main reasons why the discussion of our theory of attainment found in the introductory chapter is labelled as our conclusion, is simply that that is true. As with many anthropologists, we are driven by ethnography. The ideas behind this theory only arose when we were analysing material and writing draft chapters. We were not thinking in these terms during the ethnography. The theory of attainment was what we came to see only through endlessly peering through the lens of webcam. As with most ethnography, we work without a hypothesis. In retrospect, however, there is a clear trajectory, whereby the theory of attainment continues a discussion that was formulated in Miller and Slater (2000) some 12 years previously in their work on the initial impact of the internet on Trinidad. This became the second leg supporting our theory of attainment. Three issues dominated the composition of Miller and Slater's work. The first was their resistance to the concept of the virtual as though there was some other experience termed 'the real' to which it was opposed. That argument has largely been won, as most people today recognize online life as integral to life more generally. The book also emphasized the importance of offline alongside online research. There remains a lively debate with scholars such as Boellstorff (2008), who have demonstrated the value of such autonomous online research. In the case of webcam, such a division is in any case implausible and this volume cannot be divided between offline and online components, especially when dealing with uses of smartphones.

The third issue tackled by Miller and Slater, especially within their final chapter on religion (2000: 173–93), is about how we theorize the impact of a new medium. This proposed several labels for the dynamics of change, but as noted in the introduction to this book, the terms they chose, such as the *expansive realization*, were unfortunately clunky. In this book, we have dropped these labels but tried to retain many of the insights that they contained; for example, that people at first focus on using a new technology to overcome technical limitations and frustrations within the status quo, and only later on look at less precedented possibilities. So often, retention is the first moment in attainment. How can people who have been separated by migration to another country retain or regain their relationship? We also see more obvious examples of remediation; that is copying an earlier form of technology, with the initial use of webcam as a videophone. Only later does remediation refer to precedents in relationships rather than in media, when webcam starts to be used as always-on in order to reflect traditional modes of living together in the home. In Miller and Slater (2000), the former would have been called the *expansive realization* and the latter would have been called the *expansive potential*.

There are several advantages in moving on to a theory of attainment. But the crucial point is that these emerged through the ethnography itself. What the ethnography suggests is that retaining these two distinct stages of use as given in Miller and Slater (2000) doesn't allow us to progress fully to a more dialectical understanding. On the one hand, the first category the *expansive realization* suggests a more conservative moment, which mainly repairs and does not change us, while the final category, the *expansive potential*, is in retrospect, too suggestive of the idea of humanity becoming something new because of the new potentials in the technology.

On looking back at the ethnographic chapters within this volume, these can be used to confirm the suggestion that a population first attempts to repair what they view as precedent and then moves beyond that. But this same material fails to confirm that this results in two different kinds of consequence. The whole of our chapter on self-consciousness suggests that the most conventional way of using webcam within Skype as videocam has a possibly quite profound impact upon the way we literally see ourselves and understand who we are. While the section on always-on in the next chapter showed how in several ways this refers us back to the most conservative and domestic form of living in the home, the taken-for-granted place of co-presence within the same site. We found that always-on webcam reveals that so far from needing to communicate through the device, we create conditions of intimacy through achieving a condition in which we can relax into a comfortable state of taking each other for granted without having to say a word. By contrast, we also found that Shantel was quite uncomfortable realizing that her previous experience of co-present sex meant that most guys hadn't actually bothered talking to her. In all such cases, we are better appreciating these changes within a theory of attainment which suggests that we should not set too much store by the happenstance of historical trajectory, that we used to be unable to see ourselves as others see us, or we used not to be able to create domestic intimacy when living in different countries, or that some women had got used to having sex without the foreplay of conversation. None of these conditions are more authentic or natural than any others. They are just the assumptions we become used to given the social norms and material technologies through which we live at any particular time. What changes is merely the conventional cultural genres that make us regard a particular form of intimacy or self-expression or relationship to place as normative and taken for granted.

Let us take another example – the ethnographic discussion of relationships in Chapter Five. The study of webcam showed how, over time, relations of kin develop properties that come closer to intense friendships, while some long-term friendships develop into relationships that are more like those of kin. We also acknowledge that some relationships that are maintained through webcam would have been impossible without this medium, for example, the toddler who would not have been able to recognize and play with a grandparent through the phone, because they are too young to recognize them without visual cues. They are now connected to a grandparent where the similarity of webcam to familiar screen precedents such as television makes this more acceptable than prior forms of digital technology. None of these observations suggest that anything has changed dramatically in the nature of human relationships as a result of the technology. Rather, as in every other chapter, we have good examples of the fundamental tenets of digital anthropology. That we have gained insights into aspects of relationships that we hadn't fully appreciated before the advent of webcam put these into sharper focus. The two observations regarding the role of the visual for the very young and the elderly, and possible affinities between modes of kinship and friendship are not especially original or surprising. It's just that we now understand them better. Attainment is not a progression, but more a realization of a capacity that in retrospect simply seems an integral part of what it always could have meant to be a human being in social relationships.

When our theory of attainment was introduced in Chapter One, it came with a caveat. Just as we don't much like the word webcam, but argued it is simply the best term available; we also noted that there are weaknesses with the term 'attainment', because it implies something achieved which might overshadow more negative or contradictory consequences of webcam use. By contrast, here at the end of the volume, we see the theory of attainment not as a debate with other philosophical or theoretical concerns, but rather as a summation of our ethnographic encounter. What comes across in every single chapter is rather the way webcam is so thoroughly embedded in all aspects of everyday life. As part of polymedia, webcam is just one more mode of communication, which is likely to be simultaneously taking place on Facebook or email or phone. Similarly, self-consciousness, as discussed in relation to webcam, is merely one part of a huge concern with clothes, makeup and appearance which may re-surface every time anyone sees pretty much anyone else they know. In Chapter Five, we found webcam as only making sense if we know a great deal about each particular relationship, how that mother gets on with that daughter and with her husband.

Furthermore, attainment can also be about the failures of retainment. In the section on fathers in Chapter Five, we found that a conventional gender distinction, which worked fine when the daughter was living with them, made things worse when they tried to keep their relationship going through webcam. We have also seen how the advent of webcam as an expectation can lead elderly people, who don't use it, to feel excluded from family life. People can be rendered more homesick rather than less as a result of webcam. Parents may not particularly welcome the ability of underage schoolchildren to have cybersex, let alone have pictures of these webcam sessions later released on the internet, which certainly happens in Trinidad. Yet, all of these cases are just as much a cultural potential of webcam that has thereby been attained. This is why our use of the term attainment needs to be separated from the positive connotations of achievement. What may be *attained* may be a reiteration of traditional family quarrels, or heavily asymmetrical power relations between the genders. In retrospect, far more examples have emerged in the ethnography that would be regarded as beneficial, with webcam facilitating or fulfilling a desire. But that is not what makes these attainments. It is not the achievement of a goal, but rather the way webcam becomes embedded in what we can regard as mundane and ordinary human activity and sentiments that are testimony to attainment irrespective of whether people judge the consequence as good or bad.

What ethnography has achieved is the sense that a theory of attainment is perhaps a good deal less exciting, but perhaps a good deal more important, than it first appeared. Ethnographic evidence helps make it appear much more ordinary, and much less judgemental. We are trying to present webcam's attainments as part and parcel of personal communications. Webcam is already just what people do. As anthropologists, we view the use of technology as cultural genres. If we open up the technology, we can see the microchips and the screens – but equally present, if invisible, are the cultural wires and soldering that direct the acceptable ways for employing that technology. Because we know other peoples in other places may have a different view as to such acceptable usage, we do not see inevitability or determinism. It is the ethnography that explains what we meant when we argued that our theory of attainment is intended to bring technology studies back within the embrace of anthropology more generally.

This point was first established in Chapter Two through our initial extended case study of Colin. We noted there that there were three possible levels of accounting for what was rather extreme behaviour in using two screens and endlessly preening himself. We could have dismissed him as merely an eccentric individual; we could have used some universal psychology of self-consciousness. But the details of his case showed why neither would do. Much of the discussion related to the way people perform themselves around very specific genres, for example, what in Trinidad used to be called *picong* but is now called shit-talk. This is neither individual nor universal. In every single chapter, the main context for understanding webcam is through understanding cultural genres, rather than psychology – what is expected of friends in Trinidad, the relationship between BBM and intimacy, homes that have little regard for what in other countries would be seen as essential privacy. The study of webcam as attainment shows how cultural diversity grows in some areas while it shrinks in others. Nothing in this volume was inevitable, and comparative studies may show quite different consequences. A theory of attainment is not then the achievement of something intrinsic; it is the opposite – an anthropological acceptance that we continue to proliferate diversity in the creativity we bring to each and every technological development.

By this stage, we can see how a theory of attainment is in some ways just a re-statement of the premise of anthropology. A tribe in New Guinea may practise rituals that seem bizarre to outsiders, but to insiders it's merely our 'custom', what any proper human being should do. Anthropology is the acceptance of the synchronic diversity of humanity. It was born in the refusal of evolutionary theory that might have implied that some people are more biologically advanced or better adapted than some others. Wherever you go, people are different, not because some are more evolved, but because culture is extraordinarily creative and our cosmologies enormously diverse. The theory of attainment applies the exact same anthropological principle to a diachronic rather than this synchronic dimension. Technological development already seems to grow exponentially. If we were able to meet humanity in a few centuries time with all that further technological development, it is likely that those people will seem far more bizarre than our contemporaries in New Guinea or for that matter in California. We must also acknowledge that our period of history will seem equally bizarre to them. From their perspective, these technologies have merely enabled them to attain what they will regard as what was always the ordinary potential in simply being human. They will probably be having the same debates about whether their children are being properly socialized and the thousand moral issues that beset us. Their discussions about what should be called human or post-human will by then have become fiendishly complex, but they will likely be debating them in a similar way to ourselves. For anthropology, the future is merely our equal. Neither a brighter beginning nor a lost past, the future will be just another example of us.

References

Abrahams, R.D. (1983) *The Man-Of-Words in the West Indies: Performance and the Emergence of Creole Culture*, Baltimore, MD: Johns Hopkins University Press.

Abu-Lughod, L. (1998) *Remaking Women: Feminism and Modernity in the Middle East*, Princeton, NJ: Princeton University Press.

Ahearn, L. (2001) *Invitations to Love: Literacy, Love Letters, and Social Change in Nepal*, Ann Arbor, MI: University of Michigan Press.

Alavi, K., Sail, R.M., Mohamad, M.S., Omar, M., Subhi, N., Chong, S.T., Sarnon, N., Fauziah, I. and Lukman, Z.M. (2011) 'Exploring the Meaning of Ageing and Quality of Life for the Sub-Urban Older People', *Pertanika Journal of Social Sciences and Humanities*, 19, 41–8.

Allan, G.A. (1989) *Friendship: Developing a Sociological Perspective*, Hemel Hempstead: Harvester Wheatsheaf.

Ashton, K. (2009) 'That "Internet of Things" Thing', *RFID Journal*, 22 June. http://www.rfidjournal.com/article/view/4986 (accessed 10 February 2013).

Bajic, I. (2009) 'Unmaking Family Relationships: Belgrade Mothers and their Migrant Children', in Miller, D. (ed.), *Anthropology and the Individual: A Material Culture Perspective*, Oxford: Berg.

Barlow, K. and Chapin, B. (2010) The Practice of Mothering: An Introduction', *Ethos: Journal of the Society for Psychological Anthropology*, 38 (4), 324–38.

Barthes, R. (1977) 'Rhetoric of the Image', in Heath, S. (ed. and trans.), *Image, Music, Text*, New York: Hill and Wang, pp. 32–51.

Basu, P. (2007) *Highland Homecomings: Genealogy and Heritage-Tourism in the Scottish Diaspora*, London: Routledge.

Baym, N. (2010) *Personal Connections in the Digital Age*, Cambridge: Polity.

Beck, U. and Beck-Gernsheim, E. (1995) *The Normal Chaos of Love*, Frankfurt: Polity.

Behrend, H. (2003) 'Photo Magic: Photographs in Practices of Healing and Harming in East Africa', *Journal of Religion in Africa*, 33, 129–45.

Bell, S. and Coleman, S. (eds) (1999) *The Anthropology of Friendship*, Oxford: Berg.

Ben-Ze'ev, A. (2004) *Love Online: Emotions on the Internet*, Cambridge: Cambridge University Press.

Bergson, H. (2007 [1912]) *Matter and Memory*, New York: Cosimo.

Bernhardt, T. and Milberg, W. (2011) 'Does Economic Upgrading Generate Social Upgrading? Insights from the Horticulture, Apparel, Mobile Phones and Tourism Sectors', Capturing the Gains Working Paper No. 2011/07, http://papers.ssrn.com/sol3/papers.cfm?abstract_id=1987694 (accessed 10 February 2013).

Boellstorff, T. (2008) *Coming of Age in Second Life*. Princeton, NJ: Princeton University Press.

Bolter, J.D. and Grusin, R. (2000) *Remediation: Understanding New Media*, Cambridge, MA: MIT Press.

Botticello, J. (2009) 'Fashioning Individuality and Social Connectivity among Yoruba Women in London', in Miller, D. (ed.), *Anthropology and the Individual: A Material Culture Perspective*, Oxford: Berg.

Bourdieu, P. (1977) *Outline of a Theory of Practice*, Cambridge: Cambridge University Press.

Bourdieu, P. (1984) *Distinction: A Social Critique of the Judgment of Taste* (tr. Nice, R.), London: Routledge.

Bowlby, J. (1988) *A Secure Base: Parent–Child Attachment and Healthy Human Development*, New York: Basic Books.

boyd, d. (2013) 'Networked Privacy', *Surveillance & Society*, 10, 348–50.

Brickell, K. (2011) '"Mapping" and "Doing" Critical Geographies of Home', *Progress in Human Geography*, 36 (2), 225–44.

Broadbent, S. (2011) *L'intimité au travail (Intimacy at work – The emergence of the private sphere and private communications in the enterprise)*, Limoges: FYP Editions.

Broadbent, S. (2012) 'Approaches to Personal Communications', in Horst, H. and Miller, D. (eds), *Digital Anthropology*, London: Berg.

Brosnan, M.J. (1998) *Technophobia: The Psychological Impact of Information Technology*, New York: Routledge.

Buber, M. (2000) *I and Thou*, New York: Scribner Press.

Burrell, J. (2012) *Invisible Users: Youth in the Internet Cafés of Urban Ghana*, Cambridge, MA: MIT Press.

Carsten, J. (2007) 'Constitutive Knowledge: Tracing Trajectories of Information in New Contexts of Relatedness', *Anthropological Quarterly*, 80 (2), 403–26.

Carsten, J. (2003) *After Kinship*, Cambridge: Cambridge University Press.

Carter, D. (2008) 'The Gift in Cyberspace', *Anthropology in Action*, 15 (3), 22–33.

Chamberlain, M. (2003) 'Rethinking Caribbean Families: Extending the Links', *Community, Work and Family*, 6 (1), 63–76.

Chevannes, B. (2001) *Learning to be a Man: Culture, Socialization, and Gender Identity in Five Caribbean Communities*, Cave Hill: University of the West Indies Press.

Chu, J. (2010) *Cosmologies of Credit: Transnational Mobility and the Politics of Destination in China*. Durham, NC: Duke University Press.

Cicirelli, V.G. (1995) *Sibling Relationships across the Life Span*, New York: Plenum Press.

Clarke, A. (2001) 'The Aesthetics of Social Aspiration', in Miller, D. (ed.), *Home Possessions*, Oxford: Berg.

Clarke, E. (1999) *My Mother Who Fathered Me: A Study of the Families in Three Selected Communities of Jamaica*, Kingston: University of the West Indies Press.

Cohen, A.P. (1994) *Self-Consciousness: An Alternative Anthropology of Identity*, London: Routledge.

Collier, J. (1997) *From Duty to Desire: Remaking Families in a Spanish Village*, Princeton, NJ: Princeton University Press.

Conradson, D. and Latham, A. (2005) 'Friendship, Networks and Transnationality in a World City: Antipodean Transmigrants in London', *Journal of Ethnic and Migration Studies*, 31 (2), 287–305.

Dalakoglou, D. (2009) 'Building and Ordering Transnationalism: The "Greek House" in Albania as a Material Process', in Miller, D. (ed.), *Anthropology and the Individual: A Material Culture Perspective*, Oxford: Berg.

Donner, H. (2012) 'Love and Marriage, Globally', *Anthropology of This Century*, No. 4, May, http://aotcpress.com/articles/love-marriage-globally/.

Durkheim, E. (1993) *The Division of Labour in Society*, New York: The Free Press.

Edwards, R., Hadfield, L., Lucey, H. and Mauthner, M. (2006) *Sibling Identity and Relationships: Sisters and Brothers*, Abingdon: Routledge.

Fernandes, J. (1991) 'Sex into Sexuality: A Feminist Agenda for the '90s', *Art Journal*, 50 (2), 35–8.
Flaubert, G. (1996) *Madame Bovary*, New York: Doubleday.
Fortunati, L., Pertierra, R. and Vincent, J. (eds) (2012) *Migration, Diaspora and Information Technology in Global Societies*, London: Routledge.
Fox, K. (2004) *Watching the English: The Hidden Rules of English Behaviour*, London: Hodder & Stoughton.
Fu, P. (2010) 'Digital Kinship: Ethnography on Digital Practice of Families in Shanghai', Master's dissertation, London: University College London.
Fukuyama, F. (2003) *Our Posthuman Future: Consequences of the Biotechnology Revolution*, New York: Farrar, Straus and Giroux.
Fulk, J. (1993) 'Social Constriction of Communication Technology', *Academy of Management Journal*, 36, 921–50.
Gammeltoft, T. (2003) 'The Ritualisation of Abortion in Contemporary Vietnam', *The Australian Journal of Anthropology*, 14 (12), 129–43.
Garvey, P. (2001) 'Organised Disorder: Moving Furniture in Norwegian Homes', in Miller, D. (ed.), *Home Possessions*, Oxford: Berg.
Gates, D. (1990) 'Decoding Rap Music', *Newsweek*, 19 March, pp. 60–3.
Gershon, I. (2010) *The Break-Up 2.0: Disconnecting over New Media*, Ithaca, NY: Cornell University Press.
Giddens, A. (1991) *Modernity and Self-Identity: Self and Society in the Late Modern Age*, Stanford, CA: Stanford University Press.
Gilsenan, M. (2005) *Recognising Islam: Religion and Society in the Modern Middle East*, London: I.B. Tauris.
Godelier, M. (2012) *The Metamorphosis of Kinship*, London: Verso Books.
Goffman, E. (1959) *The Presentation of Self in Everyday Life*, New York: Doubleday.
Goffman, E. (1975) *Frame Analysis*, Harmondsworth: Penguin.
Gonzalez, N. (1984) 'Rethinking the Consanguineal Household and Matrifocality', *Ethnology*, 13, 1–12.
Goody, J. (1977) *The Domestication of the Savage Mind*, Cambridge: Cambridge University Press.
Goody, J. (1987) *The Interface between the Written and the Oral*, Cambridge: Cambridge University Press.
Greschke, H.M. (2012) *Is There a Home in Cyberspace? The Internet in Migrants' Everyday Life and the Emergence of Global Communities*, New York: Routledge.
Halbwachs, M. (1992) *On Collective Memory*, Chicago, IL: University of Chicago Press.

Hand, S. (ed.) (1989) *The Levinas Reader*, Oxford: Blackwell.

Haraway, D. (1991) *Simians, Cyborgs and Women: The Reinvention of Nature*, New York: Routledge.

Hayden, D. (1981) *The Grand Domestic Revolution*, Cambridge, MA: MIT Press.

Hewlett, B.S. (1991) *Intimate Fathers, The Nature and Context of Aka Pygmy Paternal Infant Care*, Ann Arbor, MI: University of Michigan Press.

Hirsch, J. and Wardlow, H. (eds) (2006) *Modern Loves: The Anthropology of Romantic Courtship and Companionate Marriage*, Ann Arbor, MI: University of Michigan Press.

Ho, C. (1993) 'The Internationalization of Kinship and the Feminization of Caribbean Migration: The Case of Afro-Trinidadian Immigrants in Los Angeles', *Human Organization*, 52 (1), 32–40.

Hockey, J. (2002) 'Interviews as Ethnography? Disembodied Social Interaction in Britain', in Rapport, N. (ed.), *British Subjects: An Anthropology of Britain*, Oxford: Berg.

Horst, H. (2009) 'Aesthetics of the Self: Digital Mediations', in Miller, D. (ed.), *Anthropology and the Individual: A Material Culture Perspective*, Oxford: Berg, pp. 99–113.

Horst, H. and Miller, D. (2006) *The Cell Phone: An Anthropology of Communication*, Oxford: Berg.

Horst, H. and Miller, D. (eds) (2012) *Digital Anthropology*, London: Berg.

Horst, H., Martinez, K. and Sima, C. (2010) 'Families', in Ito, M. (ed.), *Hanging Out, Messing Around and Geeking Out: Kids Living and Learning with New Media*, Cambridge, MA: MIT Press.

Hoskins, J. (2009) 'The Camera as Global Vampire: The Distorted Mirror of Photography in Remote Indonesia and Elsewhere', in Robinson, M. and Picard, D. (eds), *The Framed World: Tourism, Tourists and Photography*, Farnham: Ashgate.

Humphrey, C. (2009) 'The Mask and the Face: Imagination and Social Life in Russian Chat Rooms and Beyond', *Ethnos*, 74, 31–50.

Hutchby, I. (2001) *Conversation and Technology: From the Telephone to the Internet*, Cambridge: Polity.

Huxley, A. (2005) *Brave New World*, New York: Harper Perennial.

Ito, M. (2009) *Engineering Play: A Cultural History of Children's Software*, Cambridge, MA: MIT Press.

Ito, M. (ed.) (2010) *Hanging Out, Messing Around and Geeking Out: Kids Living and Learning with New Media*, Cambridge, MA: MIT Press.

James, W. (1890) *The Principles of Psychology*, New York: Holt.

Jenkins, H. (2006) *Convergence Culture: Where Old and New Media Collide*, New York: NYU Press.

Kahr, B. (2007) *Sex and the Psyche*, London: Allen Lane.

Katz, J. and Aakhus, M. (eds) (2002) *Perpetual Contact: Mobile Communication, Private Talk, Public Performance*, Cambridge: Cambridge University Press.

Kaufmann, J.C. (2012) *Love Online*, Cambridge: Polity.

Kirshenblatt-Gimblett, B. (1998) *Destination Culture: Museums and Heritage*, Berkeley, CA: University of California Press.

Klass, M. (1961) *East Indians in Trinidad*, New York: Columbia University Press.

Lacan, J. (2001) *Écrits: A Selection*, London: Routledge Classics.

Lally, E. (2002) *At Home With Computers*, Oxford: Berg.

Lauer, J. (2011), 'Surveillance History and the History of New Media: An Evidential Paradigm', *New Media & Society*, 14 (4), 566–82.

Lewis, C.S. 1950 *The Lion, The Witch and the Wardrobe*, London: Geoffrey Bles.

Lieber, M. (1981) *Street Life: Afro-American Culture in Urban Trinidad*, Boston, MA: G.K. Hall.

Livingstone, S. and Haddon, L. (eds) (2009) *Kids Online: Opportunities and Risks for Children*, Bristol: The Policy Press.

Madianou, M. and Miller, D. (2012a) *New Media and Migration*, London: Routledge.

Madianou, M. and Miller, D. (2012b) 'Polymedia: Towards a New Theory of Digital Media in Interpersonal Communication', *International Journal of Cultural Studies*, 16 (2), 169–87.

Marcoux, J.S. (2001) 'The Refurbishment of Memory', in Miller, D. (ed.), *Home Possessions*, Oxford: Berg.

McCarthy, A. (2001) *Ambient Television: Visual Culture and Public Space Passions*. Durham, NC: Duke University Press.

McLuhan, M. (1964) *Understanding Media: The Extensions of Man*, New York: McGraw-Hill.

Mead, G.H. (2009 [1934]) *Mind, Self, and Society: From the Standpoint of a Social Behaviourist*, Chicago, IL: University of Chicago Press.

Melchior-Bonnet, S. (2002) *The Mirror: A History*, London: Routledge.

Mercier, J. (2012) *Skype Numerology* (blog), skypenumerology.blogspot.com (accessed 10 January 2013).

Miller, D. (1994) *Modernity: An Ethnographic Approach*, Oxford: Berg.

Miller, D. (1997) *Capitalism: An Ethnographic Approach*, Oxford: Berg.

Miller, D. (2008a) *The Comfort of Things*, Cambridge: Polity.

Miller, D. (2008b) 'What is a Relationship?', *Ethnos: Journal of Anthropology*, 72 (4), 535–54.

Miller, D. (2009a) *Stuff*, Cambridge: Polity.

Miller, D. (ed.) (2009b), *Anthropology and the Individual: A Material Culture Perspective*, Oxford: Berg.

Miller, D. (2011) *Tales From Facebook*, Cambridge: Polity.

Miller, D. and Horst, H. (2012) 'The Digital and the Human', in Horst, H. and Miller, D. (eds), *Digital Anthropology*, London: Berg, pp. 3–35.

Miller, D. and Slater, D. (2000) *The Internet: An Ethnographic Approach*, Oxford: Berg.

Miller, D. and Woodward, S. (eds) (2010) *Global Denim*, Oxford: Berg.

Miller, W. and Maiter, S. (2008) 'Fatherhood and Culture: Moving beyond Stereotypical Understandings', *Journal of Ethnic and Cultural Diversity in Social Work*, 17 (3), 279–300.

Monroe, D. (ed.) (2010) *Porn – Philosophy for Everyone: How to Think With Kink*, Malden, MA: Blackwell.

Morley, D. (2000) *Home Territories: Media, Mobility and Identity*, New York: Routledge.

Munn, N. (1973) *Walbiri Iconography*, Ithaca, NY: Cornell University Press.

Myers, F. (1986) *Pintupi Country, Pintupi Self*, Washington, DC: Smithsonian Institute Press.

Noller, P. and Fitzpatrick, M.A. (1993) *Communication in Family Relationships*, Englewood Cliffs, NJ: Prentice-Hall.

Norris, C. and Armstrong, G. (1999) *The Maximum Surveillance Society: The Rise of CCTV*, Oxford: Berg.

Oaks, L. (1994) 'Fetal Spirithood and Fetal Personhood: The Cultural Construction of Abortion in Japan', *Women's Studies International Forum*, 17 (5), 511–23.

Ong, W.J. (1982) *Orality and Literacy*, New York: Methuen.

Pahl, R. (2000) *On Friendship*, Cambridge: Polity.

Palfrey, J. and Glasser, U. (2008) *Born Digital: Understanding the First Generation of Digital Natives*, New York: Basic Books.

Parsons, T. and Bales, R.F. (1956) *Family Socialization and Interaction Process*, London: Routledge.

Peletz, M. (1995) 'Kinship Studies in Late Twentieth Century Anthropology', *Annual Review of Anthropology*, 24, 343–72.

Pertierra, R., Ugarte, E., Pingol, A., Hernandez, J. and Dacanay, N. (2002) *TXT-ING Selves: Cellphones and Philippine Modernity*, Manila: De La Salle University Press.

Piaget, J. (1999) *The Construction of Reality in the Child*, London: Routledge.

Plato (2005) *Phaedrus* (trans. Rowe, C.), London: Penguin Books.

Rainie, L. and Wellman, B. (2012) *Networked*, Cambridge, MA: MIT Press.

Rapport, N. (1997) *Transcendent Individual: Towards a Literary and Liberal Anthropology*, London: Routledge.

Rawlins, J.M., Simeon, D.T., Ramdath, D.D. and Chadee, D.D. (2008) 'The Elderly in Trinidad: Health, Social and Economic Status and Issues of Loneliness', *West Indian Medical Journal*, 57 (6), 589–95.

Rodman, H. (1971) *Lower Class Families: The Culture of Poverty in Negro Trinidad*, New York: Oxford University Press.

Rosenberg, J. (2012) 'The Secrets of Skype's Success', *TEDx Columbia Engineering*, http://www.youtube.com/watch?v=b7Vpon6RJyY (accessed 10 January 2013).

Sassatelli, R. (2010) 'Indigo Bodies: Fashion, Mirror Work and Sexual Identity in Milan', in Miller, D. and Woodward, S. (eds), *Global Denim*, Oxford: Berg.

Schama, S. (1987) *The Embarrassment of Riches: An Interpretation of Dutch Culture in the Golden Age*, New York: Vintage.

Schüll, N.W. (2012) *Addiction by Design: Machine Gambling in Las Vegas*, Princeton, NJ: Princeton University Press.

Senft, T. (2008) *Camgirls: Celebrity and Community in the Age of Social Networks*, New York: Peter Lang.

Skinner, J. (2012) *The Interview: An Ethnographic Approach*, Oxford: Berg.

Slater, D. (1998) 'Trading Sexpics on IRC: Embodiment and Authenticity on the Internet', *Body & Society*, 4 (4), 91–117.

Slater, D. and Tacchi, J. (2004) *Research on ICT Innovations for Poverty Reduction*, Paris: UNESCO.

Smart, C. and Neale, B. (1999) *Family Fragments?* Cambridge: Polity.

Socha, T.J. and Stamp, G.H. (1995) *Parents, Children and Communication: Frontiers of Theory and Research*, Hillsdale, NJ: Lawrence Erlbaum Associates.

Spyer, J. (2011) 'Making Up Art, Video and Fame: The Creation of Social Order in the Informal Realm of YouTube Beauty Gurus', Master's dissertation, London: University College London.

Strathern, M. (1979) 'The Self in Self-Decoration', *Oceania*, 44, 241–57.

Trawick, M. (1990) *Notes on Love in a Tamil Family*, Berkeley, CA: University of California Press.

Turkle, S. (1984) *The Second Self: Computers and the Human Spirit*, New York: Simon and Schuster.

Turkle, S. (2011) *Alone Together*, New York: Basic Books.

van der Geest, S. (2002) Respect and Reciprocity: Care of Elderly People in Rural Ghana, *Journal of Cross-Cultural Gerontology*, 17, 3–31.

van Dijck, J. (2007) *Mediated Memories in the Digital Age*, Stanford, CA: Stanford University Press.

Whitehead, N.L. and Wesch, M. (2012) *Human No More*, Boulder, CO: University of Colorado Press.

Wilk, R. (1989) *The Household Economy: Reconsidering the Domestic Mode of Production*, Boulder, CO: Westview Press.

Winnicott, D. (1960) 'The Theory of the Parent–Child Relationship', *International Journal of Psychoanalysis*, 41, 585–95.

Wyche, S., Schoenebeck, S. and Forte, A. (2013) 'Facebook is a Luxury': An Exploratory Study of Social Media Use in Rural Kenya, *Proceedings of ACM Conference on Computer Supported Cooperative Work and Social Computing (CSCW'13)*, San Antonio, TX.

Xiang, B. (2007) *Global 'Body Shopping': An Indian Labor System in the Information Technology Industry*, Princeton, NJ: Princeton University Press.

Yeh, S.J. and Sing, K.L. (2004) 'Living Alone, Social Support and Feeling Lonely among the Elderly', *Social Behaviour & Personality: An International Journal*, 32 (2), 129–38.

Index